1220
Ohio State Football
Trivia Q & A

ALSO BY MIKE MCGUIRE

1220
Ohio State Football
Trivia Q & A

Mike McGuire

member of

& COLLEGE HALL OF FAME, INC.

Intercollegiate Football
Researchers Association

1220
Ohio State Football
Trivia Q & A
by Mike McGuire

978-0-9772661-4-2

Published by Mike McGuire

Order copies from
Mike McGuire
27081 N. 96th Way
Scottsdale, AZ 85262
(480) 563-1424

Cover photo copyright MyTeamPrints.com
Licensed by The Ohio State University
Photo by Gregg Watson

Printed in the United States of America

American Football Booklist (AFB)

The purpose of the American Football Booklist (AFB) is to acquire, preserve, and interpret books for a collection on the subject of football. The collection was started with a commitment by the author, Mike McGuire, to donate 500 books on American football, act as the curator of the collection, and develop a website to make sure this information is available to the widest possible audience.

Book sources, such as The Library of Congress and leading bookstores confirm that there are over 8,400 titles that have been published with the keyword, "football," as of late 2007. We believe there are also several hundred other books about football where the word is not mentioned in the title. All books on the subject of American football will be targeted for the AFB collection.

A website has been registered, www.americanfootballbooklist.com, and will be active summer 2008.

At such time when the collection has grown to a substantial number, the AFB will accept applications to find a permanent library, preferably at a university or sports museum. The AFB wants the public, students, teachers, sports writers, researchers, football writers, historians, and football coaches to have full access to the collection.

How to Contribute to the AFB

Donations of historical, ex-library, antiquarian, collector's editions and current editions of football books are gladly accepted and duly noted. Any financial donations will be used for the stated purpose of the American Football Booklist. Please call for further details about becoming an AFB volunteer.

American Football Booklist (AFB)
Mike McGuire
27081 N. 96th Way
Scottsdale, AZ 85262
(480) 563-1424

Preface

I was very fortunate to start going to Ohio State football games in the "Horseshoe" in 1954 at the age of seven. My indoctrination to becoming a "Buckeye Fan" was with the Heisman winning performance of my childhood idol Howard "Hopalong" Cassady in 1955, and the blocking of Outland Trophy winner, All-American and future All-Pro Player, and inductee into the College and Pro Football Halls of Fame, Jim Parker.

I was there when the Buckeyes beat Heisman Memorial Trophy winner O.J. Simpson and the USC Trojans to win the National Championship in 1968. I was there when Heisman Memorial Trophy winner Jim Plunkett upset the Buckeyes in the 1971 Rose Bowl Game and Ohio State lost another National Championship. I was there when Archie Griffin came off the bench to run for 239 yards against North Carolina in his first college game and the start of a fabulous story of a running back who would go on to win two Heisman Memorial Trophies. I was there when freshman Eddie George fumbled twice against Illinois, but as a senior ran for 314 yards and three touchdowns against Illinois on his way to winning the Heisman Memorial Trophy. I was there when quarterback Troy Smith BEAT Michigan for the third year in a row and won the Big Ten Championship outright, advanced to the BCS National Championship and won his Heisman Memorial Trophy.

With each game and each season from the time I was a kid, the tradition, the history and the noteworthy players from Ohio State make it easy for me to state that the greatest college football program in existence today is on the banks of the Olentangy River in Columbus, Ohio in the Ohio Stadium. Ohio State football is synonymous with the term excellence!

This second expansion of the original book of *500 Ohio State Football Trivia Q & A* covers the last few years, but I have added several questions about the rules of football and more on the early days of college football. Fellow football writer Tex Noel, of 1st-N-Goal, has contributed the last 20 questions specific to Ohio State National Championships. Tex is Executive Director of the Intercollegiate Football Researchers Association; Editor, *The College Football Historian* newsletter; author of *Stars of an Earlier Autumn*; and a forthcoming book about College Football National Championships.

My purpose to continue to write trivia books about Ohio State football has stayed the same from the beginning: to enhance the reader's knowledge of the "Battling Buckeyes" and to just have some plain fun doing it. Increasing one's overall enjoyment of the history and traditions of Ohio State football is just an added benefit. Always keep your focus on "The Game," the greatest rivalry in all of college football with the University of Michigan Wolverines.

Mike McGuire

Go Bucks!™ **BEAT MICHIGAN**®

How to Use
1220 Ohio State Football Trivia Q & A

Trivia questions are always meant to be fun, tricky, thought-provoking and confusing, and to bring back good ole' memories, while testing one's knowledge of a particular subject. *1220 Ohio State Football Trivia Q & A* is no different. We do offer the following suggestions on "How to Use" the Ohio State Football Trivia Q & A book for greater enjoyment.

It is great to use as a "party starter" for any Buckeye gathering before kick-off and an excellent way to meet new people while also learning about the great traditions and history of Ohio State football. The book is laid out in a format of 20 questions and answers and Buckeye fans can go along at their own pace. Each correct answer could be worth 5 points within a group of questions, and individuals or teams awarded prizes for their skill and knowledge of Ohio State football trivia.

Tail-Gating...A great way to pass the time as the hamburgers and hotdogs are cooking on the grill. Play to see who cooks or who cleans up after the meal!

On-the-Road...Driving to and from an Ohio State game, trivia can help make the miles pass faster. Play to see who drives and who asks the questions, or who buys the next tank of gas, food, or cocktails.

On-an-Airplane, Bus or Train...A great way to study and improve your knowledge of Ohio State football traditions, history, records, players, and coaches. Upon your arrival impress your friends with your Ohio State football trivia knowledge. Maybe even meet other Ohio State fans who are traveling, too.

Local Pub or Pizza Joint...A pizza and beer always taste better with great sports trivia conversations, discussions and arguments, and it doesn't get any better than Ohio State football.

First-Date at OSU...Not highly recommended unless there is prior knowledge of the other person's love for Ohio State football.

In-the-Bathroom...OK!, but please keep the book on your night stand or a bookshelf.

Note: Handy reference material, facts and figures about Ohio State players, teams, stadiums, nicknames, bowl games, awards, websites and more are located in the back of this book.

Send me the unique ways you have used the *1200 Ohio State Football Trivia Q & A* **book.**

TABLE OF CONTENTS

QUESTIONS GROUP 1

1-1 What is the proper name of "The Horseshoe," Home of The Ohio State University Buckeyes?

1-2 What is the official Ohio State University Mascot?

1-3 Head Coach Woody Hayes coached from what season to what season?

1-4 **T or F** The OSU Faculty Council voted against the 1961 Big Ten Champions going to the Rose Bowl.

1-5 What year was Head Coach Earle Bruce inducted into the College Football Hall of Fame?

1-6 Ohio State and Michigan have met continuously since what year?

1-7 What was "The 10 Year War?"

1-8 What is the Ohio State student body cheering section called?

1-9 What is Athlon Sports No. 1 greatest college football tradition?

1-10 What game called "The Upset of the Century" was Ohio State's most costly defeat?

1-11 Who won the Outland Trophy and Lombardi Award in 1970 and is a member of the College Football Hall of Fame?

1-12 Where is the "Victory Bell" located?

1-13 Total attendance in "The Shoe" since 1922 is approximately how many million fans?

1-14 Which fullback delivered the best on Woody Hayes' philosophy "Three Yards and a Cloud of Dust?"

1-15 Name the three Ohio State players who have finished second in The Heisman Trophy voting.

1-16 How many Big Ten Championships did Woody Hayes win?

1-17 What year and which coach went 11-0 in the regular season and missed the National Championship by losing The Rose Bowl to USC 17-16?

1-18 Fullback Bob White carried the ball seven out of eight plays in a 66-yard game-winning drive to give Ohio State a Big Ten Title and a Rose Bowl trip over what team?

1-19 What was the score of the 1969 Rose Bowl game when Ohio State beat No. 1 USC Heisman Trophy winner O.J. Simpson and won the National Championship?

1-20 Archie Griffin (in his second game as a freshman) came off the bench, rushed for an Ohio State record of how many yards, and against what team?

ANSWERS GROUP 1

1-1   The Ohio Stadium
1-2   Brutus Buckeye
1-3   1951-1978
1-4   True
1-5   2003
1-6   1918
1-7   Woody Hayes vs. Bo Schembechler (1969-1978)
1-8   Block O
1-9   Dotting the "i" in Script Ohio
1-10 Michigan Game 1969, UM 24-OSU 12, OSU was a 17 point favorite
1-11 Jim Stillwagon
1-12 Southeast corner tower of Ohio Stadium
1-13 Over 35 million and quickly going to 36 million
1-14 Two-time All-American Bob Ferguson
1-15 Bob Ferguson (1961), John Hicks (1973), Keith Byars (1984)
1-16 13
1-17 1979, Head Coach Earle Bruce
1-18 Iowa, November 16, 1957
1-19 Ohio State 27, University of Southern California 16
1-20 239 yards, North Carolina, won 29-14, September 30, 1972

QUESTIONS GROUP 2

2-1 What year(s) did Woody Hayes claim the wire service National Championship?

2-2 Because the OSU vs. Michigan rivalry with Bo and Woody was so dominant in The Big Ten Conference, what was the conference called?

2-3 What year did Ohio State add the player's name on the back of their jersey?

2-4 The Ohio Stadium is located on the banks of what river?

2-5 How many Rose Bowl games did Woody Hayes' teams play in?

2-6 Who caught Craig Krensel's pass, the "Holy Buckeye," at Purdue in 2002?

2-7 **T or F** Michigan was always unbeaten going into the Ohio State game from 1972 through 1975 and only beat the Buckeyes once.

2-8 What was coach Woody Hayes' record against Michigan in 28 games?

2-9 Name the two Ohio State linebackers with the most tackles in a game.

2-10 What was the title of Woody Hayes' book published in 1969?

2-11 Name the three colleges where Woody Hayes was the head coach?

2-12 What band played the 1965 rock hit "Hang on Sloopy"?

2-13 Coach John Cooper (OSU's 21st head coach) had what record after 11 seasons?

2-14 Which game did LB Chris Spielman state was his best game?

2-15 What position did Woody Hayes play at Denison University?

2-16 Which bowl game in 1950 did Coach Hayes beat Arizona State 34-21 with his Miami of Ohio team?

2-17 Who is the "Neutron Man," known as the icon to Ohio State Football?

2-18 Where is the "Coffin Corner(s)" in Ohio Stadium?

2-19 In what year and against which opponent did the Ohio State Buckeyes play their first overtime game?

2-20 How many National Championships did Coach Jim Tressel have at Youngstown State University?

ANSWERS GROUP 2

2-1   1954, 1957, 1968

2-2   "Big 2, Little 8"

2-3   1968

2-4   The Olentangy River

2-5   Eight (including four straight from 1972-1975)

2-6   Michael Jenkins

2-7   False: they tied 10-10 in 1973

2-8   17-11-1

2-9   29 tackles, Chris Spielman (Michigan 1986), Tom Cousineau (Penn State 1978)

2-10 *Hot Line to Victory*

2-11 Denison University (1946-1948), Miami University of Ohio (1949-1950), The Ohio State University (1951-1978)

2-12 The McCoys

2-13 111-43-4

2-14 Iowa 1985, 2 interceptions, 19 tackles

2-15 Tackle

2-16 Salad Bowl

2-17 Mr. Orlas King (passed away 10-7-2004)

2-18 Both ends of the playing field between the goal line and the 10-yard line

2-19 2002, Illinois, Ohio State won 23-16

2-20 Four

QUESTIONS **GROUP 3**

3-1   **T or F**   Coach Cooper's players won the Butkus, Heisman, Lombardi, Outland and Thrope Awards.

3-2   Since 1935 the last regular season game has been with which opponent?

3-3   In honor of every OSU All-American since 1934, what is planted in "The Buckeye Grove" on the south side of Ohio Stadium?

3-4   Which head coach was an honorary "i" dotter?

3-5   What year did the "Super Sophomores" win a national championship for the Buckeyes?

3-6   John Hicks, as a senior tackle, won which two national awards?

3-7   Coach Woody Hayes referred to Michigan as what?

3-8   What was Head Coach Woody Hayes' record while coaching at Ohio State?

3-9   Who holds the record for the most rushing yards in a single game in the Horseshoe?

3-10   How many 400-yard passing games has Ohio State produced through 2004?

3-11   What is the title of the DVD about the life and times of Woody Hayes?

3-12   Who is the only kicker to win the team MVP Award?

3-13   Jack Nicklaus and Jesse Owens from Ohio State have been on the Wheaties cereal box cover. Which Big Ten coaching legend has also been so honored?

3-14   Coach Woody Hayes really had only one true peer during his coaching tenure at Ohio State, who was it?

3-15   Ohio State had five coaches in a period of eleven years. What was that time known as?

3-16   Who was voted by ESPN in 1999 as the nation's No. 1 college football recruiter?

3-17   When was coach Woody Hayes' birthday?

3-18   **T or F**   Coach Hayes' Buckeye team twice won a conference-record 17 consecutive league games.

3-19   Ohio State is the only Big Ten team to play in four consecutive Rose Bowl games. Which four seasons did Woody Hayes' team accomplish this feat?

3-20   Which Heisman Trophy Award winners wore the following numbers? #22, #40, #31, #27, #45, and #10

ANSWERS **GROUP 3**

3-1 True
3-2 The Michigan "Wolverines"
3-3 A Buckeye tree
3-4 Woody Hayes
3-5 The 1968 team
3-6 Lombardi Trophy and Outland Award
3-7 "That State up North" or "That Team up North"
3-8 1951-1978, 205-68-10, .761 winning percentage
3-9 Eddie George, 314 yards on 36 carries vs. Illinois, 1995
3-10 One, 458 yards against Florida State in 1981
3-11 *Beyond the Gridiron*
3-12 Mike Nugent, 2004
3-13 Joe Paterno, Penn State
3-14 Coach Bear Bryant, Alabama
3-15 "Graveyard of Coaches," Woody Hayes was hired and changed all of that!
3-16 Coach Bill Conley
3-17 Valentine's Day, February 14, 1913
3-18 True
3-19 1972, 1973, 1974, and 1975
3-20 Les Horvath (1944) #22, Howard "Hopalong" Cassady (1955) #40, Vic Janowicz (1950) #31, Eddie George (1995) #27, Archie Griffin (1974-75) #45, Troy Smith (2006) #10

QUESTIONS GROUP 4

4-1   **T or F**   In 1970 Ohio State was the National Football Foundation National Champion.

4-2   Coach John Cooper's last loss in the 2001 Outback Bowl to South Carolina was to which former Ohio State assistant football coach?

4-3   Which game is considered Ohio State's best victory ever?

4-4   **T or F**   The Ohio Stadium, "The Horseshoe," is listed in the National Registry of Historic Buildings.

4-5   Who stripped the Miami Hurricanes' Sean Taylor's interception and once again turned the momentum of the 2003 Fiesta Bowl National Championship Game?

4-6   Who was the last team to join The Big Ten Football Conference?

4-7   How many total victories did Coach Woody Hayes have as a college coach?

4-8   "Insight & Inspiration from Coach Earle Bruce" was the bi-line for his book titled what?

4-9   What does W.W. stand for in W.W. (Woody) Hayes' name?

4-10   What is the prestigious award that recognizes excellence in academics, athletics and community service?

4-11   What are the two Athletic Hall of Fames of which Coach Woody Hayes is a member?

4-12   Who was the first Ohio State Heisman Trophy winner to play major league baseball?

4-13   **T or F**   Coach Bo Schembechler was an assistant coach to Woody Hayes during two different periods.

4-14   **T or F**   The Big Ten representative from 1968 through 1980 (13 seasons) was either Ohio State or UM.

4-15   What is the "Skull Session?"

4-16   Which two running backs have scored five touchdowns in a single game?

4-17   What year did the Buckeyes outscore their opponents 40.2 to 7.8 and no other team came within four touchdowns of Ohio State going into the Michigan game?

4-18   Who was *The Columbus Dispatch* endorsing for the head coaching job at Ohio State in 1951?

4-19   Which Oklahoma kicker won the 1977 game 29-28 with a 41-yard field goal after the Buckeyes came back from being down 20-0 and leading 28-20?

4-20   What game cancelled Leroy Keyes' Heisman Trophy run and his team's No. 1 ranking?

ANSWERS GROUP 4

4-1   True

4-2   Lou Holtz

4-3   National Championship Game 2002, OSU 31-Miami 24 (2 OT)

4-4   True: on March 22, 1974 by the National Park Service

4-5   Maurice Clarett

4-6   Penn State

4-7   241

4-8   *Buckeye Wisdom*

4-9   Wayne Woodrow

4-10   Woody Hayes National Scholar Athlete Award

4-11   Denison Athletic Hall of Fame and College Football Hall of Fame

4-12   Vic Janowicz

4-13   True: 1952-53 (Graduate Assistant) and 1959-1963 (Assistant)

4-14   True

4-15   A concert/pep rally by the Ohio State Marching Band in St. John Arena. They start two hours before kickoff at home games.

4-16   Pete Johnson (1974 vs. North Carolina), Keith Byars (1984 vs. Illinois)

4-17   1969, but Ohio State lost 24-12

4-18   Paul Brown of the Cleveland Browns

4-19   Uwe Von Schamann

4-20   1968, Purdue, 13-0 Ohio State in the "Horseshoe"

QUESTIONS GROUP 5 *Vintage*

5-1   Who holds the Ohio State record of 10 extra points in a single game?

5-2   Who had the longest running play and did not score a touchdown in Ohio State history?

5-3   "Senior Tackle" was started in 1913 by which Head Coach?

5-4   Although over 100,000 people have probably said they were at "The Snow Bowl" game, what is the published attendance number?

5-5   Which Head Coach had the nickname "Close the Gates of Mercy?"

5-6   Who holds the rushing record for the most yards gained by a "vintage" player in a single game?

5-7   Who did Ohio State beat 23-3 in 1916 to win their first conference championship and go undefeated?

5-8   What was the "Bad Water Game?"

5-9   During the "Vintage Years" 1890-1950, how many head coaches coached seven years or more at Ohio State?

5-10 What is the least number of points scored by a "vintage" team in a bowl game?

5-11 After retiring, which Head Coach continued his career in medicine and did heart disease research?

5-12 When did Ohio State meet Michigan for the first time with The Big Ten Title on the line?

5-13 What year(s) was the first "Ramp Entrance" and "Script Ohio" by TBDBITL?

5-14 What year did Ohio State finally, after many tries, Beat Michigan?

5-15 Who was Ohio State's first All-American player in 1914?

5-16 **T or F**   Chic Harley only lettered in football as Ohio State's first three-time All-American.

5-17 What was the first game Ohio State played west of the Mississippi River?

5-18 **T or F**   Ohio State has had bad luck in winning "Stadia" games; last game at Ohio Field, Dedication games at Ohio Stadium and Michigan Stadium.

5-19 Who played his last game in the "Horseshoe," and then the next day signed with George Halas and played the last six games of 1925 with the Chicago Bears?

5-20 What "vintage" head coach had three Big Ten Championships, 16 players making All-American, and was inducted into the College Football Hall of Fame?

ANSWERS GROUP 5 *Vintage*

5-1   Vic Janowicz, 1950 vs. Iowa

5-2   Gene Fekete, 89 yards, Pittsburgh 1942

5-3   Head Coach John Wilce

5-4   50,503

5-5   Head Coach Francis Schmidt

5-6   Oliver Cline 1945, 239 yards vs. Pittsburgh

5-7   Northwestern, 1916 under Head Coach John Wilce

5-8   1942 loss at Wisconsin 17-7, when most of the Ohio State players got sick from drinking foul water on the players train, however, they still won Ohio State's first National Championship.

5-9   Two, John Wilce 16 years, Francis Schmidt seven years

5-10   Zero (0) vs. California in 1921 Rose Bowl

5-11   Dr. John Wilce, Head Coach 1913-1928

5-12   1944, Ohio State 18, Michigan 14

5-13   Ramp Entrance 1928; Script Ohio 1936

5-14   1919

5-15   Boyd Cherry

5-16   False: Chic Harley lettered in four sports... basketball, baseball, track and football.

5-17   1920 Rose Bowl, losing to California 28-0

5-18   True: Ohio State lost all three games

5-19   The Legendary Harold "Red" Grange #77

5-20   Head Coach John Wilce

QUESTIONS **GROUP 6**

6-1 Notre Dame and USC rank first with Heisman Trophy winners. Where does Ohio State rank?

6-2 What years did Coach Woody Hayes serve in the United States Navy?

6-3 "Script Ohio" is played to the rhythmic beat of what song?

6-4 How much does the "Victory Bell" weigh?

6-5 The "Tunnel of Pride" started in 1995 at the Notre Dame game was the idea of what Ex-OSU quarterback?

6-6 Which three assistant coaches for Woody Hayes are enshrined in the College Football Hall of Fame?

6-7 Who made the "Pancake" block famous?

6-8 Who was the first player to win both the Lombardi and Outland trophies in the same season?

6-9 What was head coach Woody Hayes' record in eight Rose Bowl appearances?

6-10 Which head coach won four Big Ten Titles, a Cotton Bowl and Fiesta Bowl, and was 5-4 against UM?

6-11 Which two time All-American is considered Ohio State's best pass rusher to date?

6-12 Which band member dots the "i" in Script Ohio?

6-13 What is the seating capacity of Ohio Stadium after the recent renovation, preservation and expansion?

6-14 Woody Hayes' nickname over time became what?

6-15 **T or F** Ohio State is the only school to perform "Script Ohio."

6-16 What punter holds the record for the longest punt of 74 yards at Ohio State?

6-17 What was the cost of the three-year renovation project at Ohio Stadium completed in 2001?

6-18 What corporation wanted to buy the rights and rename "The Game" (Ohio State vs. Michigan) for a million dollars in 2004?

6-19 The largest crowd to date (2006) is the 103rd game with Michigan, November 18, 2006 (42-39 OSU). What was the attendance?

6-20 Who said the following? "To be average is to be the lowest of the good and the best of the bad. Who wants to be average?"

ANSWERS GROUP 6

6-1 OSU is tied with USC and Notre Dame; all with seven winners.

6-2 1941-1946

6-3 Le Regiment

6-4 2,420 pounds

6-5 Rex Kern

6-6 Ernie Godfrey, Doyt Perry, and Earle Bruce

6-7 Orlando Pace

6-8 Jim Stillwagon, 1970

6-9 4 - 4

6-10 Earle Bruce (1979-1987)

6-11 Mike Vrabel (1993-1996)

6-12 A sousaphone player, who must be at least a fourth-year band member

6-13 101,568 seats

6-14 "The Old Man"

6-15 False: Michigan did it first, Stanford tried it and misspelled Ohio

6-16 Andy Groom

6-17 $194,000,000.00

6-18 SBC, the offer was declined!

6-19 105,708

6-20 Earle Bruce

QUESTIONS **GROUP 7**

7-1 Which three former Ohio State players are in the Top 100 Pro Football Players selection?

7-2 Who are members of all three of these: The Ohio High School, College, and Pro Football Hall of Fames?

7-3 What is a "String of Pearls?"

7-4 Head Coach Woody Hayes produced how many All-Americans?

7-5 Who holds the record for the most rushing yards at Ohio State in a single season?

7-6 Who said the following? "That victory...was for our great fans!"

7-7 Who did Ohio State defeat when Keith Byars rushed for a record 274 yards and the team came back from a 24-0 deficit?

7-8 What other Big Ten team also went undefeated in 2002 to share the Big Ten Title with Ohio State?

7-9 Who was the first Ohio State sophomore player to ever win the Lombardi Trophy?

7-10 Who was Ohio State's first two-time All-American linebacker?

7-11 **T or F** The "Super Sophomores" did not lose a game in "The Horseshoe" for three years.

7-12 Who was the first player to be taken as the first pick in the NFL Draft from Ohio State?

7-13 What was Woody Hayes' worst home defeat at Ohio State?

7-14 Who was Woody Hayes' secondary coach on the 1968 National Championship team?

7-15 Which two All-American tackles did fullback Jim Otis run behind?

7-16 Head coach Jim Tressel played what position at Baldwin-Wallace?

7-17 Which Michigan player "Flaunted" the Heisman Trophy pose in "The Game"?

7-18 Who said the following? "The thing I'm most proud of about my college career is that I played on four teams that never lost to Michigan."

7-19 Who caught Craig Krenzel's winning touchdown pass on 4th-and-1 with 1:36 left to play at Purdue in 2002?

7-20 Who scored the first touchdown for first year Head Coach Woody Hayes in 1951?

ANSWERS GROUP 7

7-1   Lou "the toe" Groza, Jim Parker, and Paul Warfield

7-2   Jim Parker and Bill Willis

7-3   Missed tacklers left in the line of the running back. Archie Griffin was very good at this!

7-4   56

7-5   Eddie George, 1,927 yards, 1995

7-6   John Cooper, 1997 Rose Bowl (Ohio State 20-Arizona State 17)

7-7   Illinois, 1984 (Ohio State 45-Illinois 38)

7-8   Iowa "Hawkeyes"

7-9   Orlando Pace

7-10   Dwight "Ike" Kelly 1964-1965

7-11   True! As a team they were 27-2 for three years

7-12   Tom Cousineau, 1979

7-13   Purdue, 41-6 home loss in 1967

7-14   Lou Holtz

7-15   Dave Foley and Rufus Mayes

7-16   Quarterback

7-17   Desmond Howard, 1991

7-18   Archie Griffin, 1972-1975

7-19   Michael Jenkins

7-20   Robert "Rock" Joslin

QUESTIONS **GROUP 8**

8-1 Which Wolverine QB has thrown a touchdown pass in Super Bowl #38 and #39 to which former Ohio State Buckeye defensive player?

8-2 What do players and coaches receive following the victories over the Michigan Wolverines?

8-3 The Ohio Stadium is located on what road?

8-4 Who said the following? "You win with people."

8-5 Six of the Top 10 Ohio State records for passing yards in a single game are held by which quarterback?

8-6 Who came through unblocked to block a Michigan punt in the 4th quarter and then the ball was picked up by Todd Bell, who ran it in for the game winning touchdown?

8-7 Buckeye Spirit Song, "We Don't Give a Damn for The Whole State of _____?"

8-8 Which player led the Buckeyes in tackles for three years in the 1990s?

8-9 Who led Ohio State in rushing in 1967, '68 and '69, with career totals of 2,542 yards and 35 touchdowns?

8-10 Jim Otis scored four touchdowns against Michigan in 1968 giving him 16 for the season. Whose record did he break?

8-11 Which two quarterbacks filled "in relief" for Rex Kern when he was hurt during the National Championship run in 1968?

8-12 Which All-American quarterback started 48 consecutive games?

8-13 Who said the following? "He's a better young man than he is a football player, and he's the best football player I've ever seen."

8-14 **T or F** The Ohio State Buckeyes have been called "Defensive Back U."

8-15 Which quarterback, in his final game against Michigan, threw for 330 yards and three touchdowns?

8-16 Who did play-by-play from 1950 to 1979 for radio, served as assistant SID (1949-1972), and was the Sports Information Director (SID) from 1973 until his retirement in 1987?

8-17 Name the six former Ohio State players in the NFL Hall of Fame.

8-18 Which Ohio State quarterback is the career passing leader in yards?

8-19 **T or F** Three Ohio State quarterbacks have a career completion percentage over 60%.

8-20 Which two Buckeye quarterbacks have thrown five touchdown passes in a game?

ANSWERS GROUP 8

8-1   Tom Brady and Mike Vrabel

8-2   A gold charm of a pair of football pants

8-3   411 Woody Hayes Drive, Columbus, Ohio 43210

8-4   Woody Hayes, it's the title of his second book

8-5   Joe Germaine, 1997 and 1998

8-6   Jim Laughlin, sending the No. 1 Buckeyes to the Rose Bowl

8-7   Michigan

8-8   Steve Tovar 1990-91-92

8-9   Jim Otis

8-10 Howard "Hopalong" Cassady

8-11 Bill Long and Ron Maciejowski

8-12 Art Schlichter 1978-1981

8-13 Woody Hayes about Archie Griffin

8-14 True: but what about "Wide Receiver U" and replacing Penn State as "Linebacker U"

8-15 Joe Germaine, 1998

8-16 Marv Homan

8-17 Sid Gillman, Lou Groza, Dante Lavelli, Jim Parker, Paul Warfield, and Bill Willis

8-18 Art Schlichter, 7,547 yards, 1978-1981

8-19 False: one quarterback has done it. Troy Smith 63.4%

8-20 Bobby Hoying, (two times) 1994-1995 and John Borton, 1952

QUESTIONS GROUP 9

9-1 He won two Lombardi Awards ('95 and '96) and an Outland Trophy ('96) before becoming the No. 1 overall draft pick in the NFL. Who was he?

9-2 By many historians, who is considered the greatest athlete ever at The Ohio State University?

9-3 In what year did the Big Ten Athletic Directors vote to send Ohio State to the Rose Bowl after a 10-10 tie with the undefeated Michigan Wolverines?

9-4 Which All-American Ohio State tackle was the first full-time offensive lineman named to the Pro Football Hall of Fame?

9-5 When is Bo Schembechler's birthday?

9-6 The Ohio State rushing yards record for a career is held by which running back?

9-7 Through 2006, what is Ohio State's home opening game record?

9-8 Who holds the Ohio State record for career interceptions at 22?

9-9 What was the smallest crowd after the 1950 "Snow Bowl?"

9-10 Who said the following? "The greatest defensive effort I've ever seen."

9-11 After winning their fifth Big Ten Title in six years, Columbus was called what?

9-12 What father/son combination were both Co-Captains at Ohio State?

9-13 Of all the wonderful honors Coach Woody Hayes received, what did he consider the greatest?

9-14 Who said the following? "The greatest comeback after the worst start I've ever been associated with."

9-15 Which All-American punter holds the Ohio State punting average record of 45.0 yards on 109 punts?

9-16 Who holds the Ohio State record for the most punt return yardage in a single game?

9-17 **T or F** Art Schlichter was 4th, 6th, and 5th in 1979, 1980 and 1981 in the Heisman Trophy voting.

9-18 Through 2006 when opponents were ranked No. 1, what was Ohio State's win/loss record?

9-19 What is "The Pride of the Buckeyes?"

9-20 Who is the only Buckeye running back to lead his teams in rushing yards in four straight seasons?

ANSWERS GROUP 9

9-1 Orlando Pace
9-2 Vic Janowicz
9-3 1973; Bo was HOT!
9-4 Jim Parker
9-5 April Fools' Day, April 1, 1929
9-6 Archie Griffin, 5,589 yards, 1972-1975
9-7 104-7-4
9-8 Mike Sensibaugh
9-9 11-11-1967, Wisconsin, in a downpour. 65,470 fans
9-10 Woody Hayes after beating No. 1 Purdue 13-0 in 1968
9-11 "The Capital of College Football"
9-12 Jim Herbstreit, 1960 and Kirk Herbstreit, 1992
9-13 Delivering the Commencement Address at Ohio State, March 22, 1986
9-14 Earle Bruce, Illinois 1984, Ohio State won 45-38
9-15 Andy Groom
9-16 Neal Colzie, 170 yards vs. Michigan State 1973
9-17 True
9-18 6 - 9
9-19 The Ohio State University Marching Band. All Brass Band of 225 proud members.
9-20 Archie Griffin

QUESTIONS GROUP 10 *Vintage*

10-1 Who was Ohio State's first three-time All-American?

10-2 On what date was the Ohio Stadium dedicated and who was the opponent that day?

10-3 What was the name of the football field Ohio State played on before building "The Horseshoe?"

10-4 The site where the new Ohio Stadium was to be built was known as what?

10-5 **T or F** Ohio State won the Michigan Stadium dedication game October 22, 1927.

10-6 Which head coach won the first National Football Championship for the Ohio State Buckeyes?

10-7 **T or F** Ohio State did not win the Michigan game until their 16th meeting in 1919.

10-8 The Ohio State fight song "Across the Field" was written as a tribute to which head coach?

10-9 What was the date of the famous "Snow Bowl?"

10-10 Who was Maudine Ormsby?

10-11 Who is credited with being the "Father of the Ohio Stadium" project in the 1920s?

10-12 Which school colors were picked before Scarlet & Gray...as no one had these colors?

10-13 What was the seating capacity of the new Ohio Stadium in 1922?

10-14 Who was the Athletic Director during the construction of the Ohio Stadium?

10-15 Before it was renamed The Ohio Field in 1908, what was the previous football field called?

10-16 Head Coach Wes Fesler's last game was against whom?

10-17 Ohio State's airport on Case Road in Columbus, Ohio is named after which former player?

10-18 Which Ohio State All-American fullback became the Buckeyes' baseball coach from 1951 to 1975?

10-19 Who holds the Ohio State record for the most extra points in a "vintage" game?

10-20 He only played three college games for Head Coach Paul Brown, but he made the NFL Hall of Fame as a Cleveland Brown. Who was he?

ANSWERS GROUP 10 *Vintage*

10-1   Charles Wesley "Chic" Harley 1916, 1917 and 1919
10-2   October 21, 1922, Michigan "Wolverines"
10-3   Ohio Field
10-4   "Cricket Land"
10-5   False: Ohio State lost 21-0
10-6   Paul Brown, 1942
10-7   True
10-8   John Wilce, 1913-1928
10-9   November 25, 1950
10-10 Homecoming Queen 1926, actually she was a Holstein dairy cow
10-11 Professor Thomas French, Engineering Department Chairman
10-12 Orange and Black, but Princeton already had these colors
10-13 66,210
10-14 Lynn St. John
10-15 University Field
10-16 1950 Michigan in "The Snow Bowl," Head Coach Fesler's record was 0-3-1 vs. Michigan
10-17 Don Scott, Quarterback 1938-39-40
10-18 Marty Karow
10-19 Vic Janowicz, 1950 vs. Iowa
10-20 Dante Lavelli, nicknamed "gluefingers"

QUESTIONS **GROUP 11**

11-1   The Ohio State records for rushing yards in a single game for 1st and 2nd place are held against the same opponent. Who is that opponent?

11-2   The Buckeyes attempted an unusual play for them in the first half of the National Championship Game against the Miami Hurricanes. What was it?

11-3   Which Buckeye holds the records for both single season and career sacks?

11-4   In "The Super Sophomores" class of 1967, how many were drafted into the NFL?

11-5   From 1890, including present day Coach Jim Tressel, how many head coaches has Ohio State had?

11-6   In 1951, when new Head Coach Woody Hayes arrived, he changed the offense from a single wing to what new formation?

11-7   Whose number was the first to be retired in the "Horseshoe?"

11-8   What is the "Illibuck?"

11-9   Who holds the NCAA record with a career average of 6.13 yards per carry?

11-10   What was the title of the bestselling book by Ohio State All-American Jack Tatum?

11-11   Which head coach gave the now famous "310 Days" speech?

11-12   Who said the following? "It's always hard to lose, but I don't mind it as much today because of all you've been through."

11-13   Which Ohio State linebacker is the only winner of the Butkus Award?

11-14   What award is for a lineman (either side of the ball) or a linebacker no further than five yards deep?

11-15   Astro Turf and Super Turf have been two artificial surfaces in the Ohio Stadium. What is the current grass called?

11-16   As of 2004, how many major individual awards have Ohio State players won?

11-17   Name the Ohio State "Band Center" in the Ohio Stadium.

11-18   **T or F**   The Buckeye Nut is a shiny, dark brown nut with a light tan patch that resembles the eye of a deer and carrying one brings good luck.

11-19   How many school records did two-time All-American kicker Mike Nugent set in his career?

11-20   How many 100-yard rushing games did Ohio State have in 2004?

ANSWERS GROUP 11

11-1   Illinois, 314 yards 1995, 274 yards 1984

11-2   Fake Field Goal, which failed

11-3   Mike Vrabel, 13 in a single season 1995, 36 career

11-4   13

11-5   22

11-6   T-Formation

11-7   #45 Archie Griffin, 10-30-1999

11-8   A wooden turtle trophy awarded to the Ohio State-Illinois winner since 1925

11-9   Archie Griffin

11-10   *They Call Me Assassin*

11-11   New Head Coach Jim Tressel

11-12   Bo Schembechler to Earle Bruce, after Ohio State upset Michigan 1987

11-13   Andy Katzenmoyer

11-14   Lombardi Award

11-15   FieldTurf, installed in 2007

11-16   30

11-17   Steinbrenner Band Center

11-18   True

11-19   21

11-20   2

QUESTIONS GROUP 12

12-1   **T or F**   Linebacker Andy Katzenmoyer lead the team in tackles his sophomore and junior years.

12-2   After the renovation of The Ohio Stadium with 101,568 seats, where does it rank in size in regards to other stadiums?

12-3   Which head coach called the trick play "fumbleroski" in the Michigan game?

12-4   Who said the following? "Coaching is nothing more than eliminating mistakes before you get fired."

12-5   What kicker "hit" four field goals to beat Michigan in 1974, 12-10?

12-6   Who "ran blocked" for Hopalong Cassady, and "pass blocked" for Johnny Unitas?

12-7   The Michigan Stadium is called what?

12-8   What was the "No Repeat" rule?

12-9   Who was the first true freshman to start at running back after World War II?

12-10   What Ohio State running back has the record for the most 100-yard games in a season?

12-11   What does "Old Button Shoe" mean?

12-12   Which Ohio State player won the Fred Bilentnikoff Award for the best collegiate receiver?

12-13   Which Ohio State team had the most All-Americans?

12-14   Who holds the Ohio State record for total offense against Michigan in a single game?

12-15   Which Ohio State Head Coach has scored the most points against Michigan in a game?

12-16   Which Athletic Director at Ohio State played halfback and quarterback at Michigan?

12-17   Since 1950, how many times have Ohio State and Michigan tied (shared) the Big Ten Title?

12-18   Before Woody Hayes won (17-0) at Ann Arbor in 1955, how many years had it been since the last victory for the Buckeyes in Michigan Stadium?

12-19   How many running backs have rushed for over 3000 yards in their careers at Ohio State?

12-20   Who holds the Ohio State record for the most passing yards (3,330) in a single season?

ANSWERS GROUP 12

12-1   False: Katzenmoyer never led the defensive team in tackles

12-2   Fourth. Michigan is first with 107,501 seats, Tennessee second and Penn State third.

12-3   Head Coach Earle Bruce, with Jim Lachey the pulling guard

12-4   Lou Holtz

12-5   Tom Klaban, 47, 25, 43 and 45 yards

12-6   All-American, All-Pro Jim Parker

12-7   "The Big House"

12-8   No team in the Big Ten Conference could go to the Rose Bowl in back-to-back years

12-9   Maurice Clarett

12-10   Eddie George at 12, Archie Griffin twice had 11 games (Archie played fewer games each year)

12-11   T-Formation, with a full house backfield, per coach Woody Hayes

12-12   Terry Glenn, 1995

12-13   1974, DeCree, Schumacher, Cusick, Myers, Griffing, Colzie, and Skladany

12-14   Quarterback Troy Smith, 386 yards, 2004

12-15   Woody Hayes, twice 50 points...1961 and 1968

12-16   Rick Bay, 1961-1964 at the University of Michigan, he did not earn a letter, AD 1984-1987

12-17   Eight times

12-18   18 years...1937 by Francis Schmidt

12-19   Five, Griffin, George, Spencer, Byars and Pearson

12-20   Joe Germaine, 1998

QUESTIONS GROUP 13

13-1 Who said the following? "You've been great, but to be great at Ohio State you've got to Beat Michigan."

13-2 After the 2004 season, who was Ohio State's all-time leading scorer?

13-3 What was Archie Griffin's best overall rushing effort?

13-4 After the 1969 upset loss to Michigan, a custom-made rug was located outside the locker room by head coach Woody Hayes that said what?

13-5 Who said the following? "I think every Buckeye who plays their last game in the Horseshoe leaves something of themselves out there. It's part of playing at Ohio State."

13-6 Jack Nicklaus, the world's greatest golfer went to Pharmacy School at Ohio State. Who is the only player to play in the Rose Bowl and on a National Championship team that is a pharmacist?

13-7 Which of Head Coach Woody Hayes' players is a three-time Academic All-American?

13-8 How many coaches at Ohio State have been inducted into the College Football Hall of Fame?

13-9 What year between 1991 and 1999 did Ohio State not have a first round NFL draft pick?

13-10 Ohio State has had seven Heisman Trophy winners since 1936. How many has Michigan had?

13-11 Which two Ohio State players hold the record for touchdowns (points) in a Michigan game?

13-12 Who was a three year starter at center for Ohio State (1960-62) and head coach at Michigan (1990-94)?

13-13 Which Ohio State team was the first in the NCAA 1A Division to win 14 games in a season?

13-14 Which Ohio State quarterback has the most touchdown passes in a single season?

13-15 How many Ohio State receivers have had 1000 yards in receptions in a single season?

13-16 Which Ohio State player has had three pass interceptions in one game against Michigan?

13-17 **T or F** The "wolverine" is not a native animal of the State of Michigan.

13-18 Which receiver is the leading career receiver in yardage at Ohio State?

13-19 Which receiver holds the Ohio State record for the most receptions in a career?

13-20 Which two Ohio State rushing backs hold the record for rushing touchdowns in a single game?

ANSWERS GROUP 13

13-1   Earle Bruce, Senior Tackle, 1996

13-2   Kicker Mike Nugent, 356 points

13-3   246 yards, 30 carries, 11-17-1973 vs. Iowa

13-4   1969 Michigan 24, OSU 12, 1970 Mich. ____, OSU____.

13-5   Linebacker Matt Wilhelm, 2002, Ohio State 14, Michigan 9

13-6   Tom Bartley #35, Linebacker 1968, Bartley's Pharmacy, Waverly, Ohio

13-7   Dave Foley, 1966-67-68

13-8   Eight. Jones, Wilce, Schmidt, Godfrey, Hayes, Gillman, Perry, and Bruce

13-9   1998

13-10   Three. Tom Harmon (1940), Desmond Howard (1991) and Charles Woodson (1997)

13-11   24 points, four touchdowns: Bob Ferguson (1961), Jim Otis (1968)

13-12   Gary Moeller, Co-Captain 1962

13-13   2002

13-14   Troy Smith, 30, 2006

13-15   Four. Jenkins (2002), Carter (1986), Glenn (1995), and Boston (1998)

13-16   Fred Bruney, 1952

13-17   True: not a verifiable trapping in the whole state of Michigan

13-18   Michael Jenkins, 2,898 yards, 2000-2003

13-19   David Boston, 191, 1996-1998

13-20   Pete Johnson, North Carolina 1974, Keith Byars, Illinois 1984; five TDs each

QUESTIONS GROUP 14

14-1   Which two Buckeye quarterbacks passed for over 1,000 yards in the same season?

14-2   Who said the following? "This is the greatest team I've ever coached. I never saw a team play so close to perfection. You never let up."

14-3   Who is the only player in Big Ten history to play on three undisputed league champion teams?

14-4   Name the two greatest interceptions returned for touchdowns by Buckeyes in Ohio Stadium.

14-5   Name the only Ohio State kicker to win the Lou Groza Award.

14-6   Where are pictures of current and former Buckeye players displayed in the Ohio Stadium?

14-7   How many interceptions did Rex Kern throw in the 1969 "upset loss" to Michigan?

14-8   What is the individual Ohio State record for total tackles in a Michigan game?

14-9   **T or F**   QB Art Schlichter had 50 touchdown passes in his career at Ohio State, and is the most by any quarterback.

14-10   How many quarterbacks have thrown for over 5,000 yards in their career at Ohio State?

14-11   Who is the Ohio State career total offense leader?

14-12   **T or F**   There has been a player who averaged over 200 all-purpose yards per game for a single season.

14-13   Which two Ohio State kickers have kicked five field goals in a single game?

14-14   Who holds the record at Ohio State of 211 total tackles in a single season?

14-15   What year did home attendance in the "Horseshoe" pass the "half-a-million" mark?

14-16   Who was the leading tackler on the 2002 National Championship team?

14-17   What was Head Coach John Cooper's 13-year record against Michigan?

14-18   UM running back Tshminanga Biakabutuka, a.k.a. "Tim" rushed for how many yards (a record) to win against Ohio State in 1995?

14-19   UM player Tai Streets caught a 68-yard touchdown pass when Big Ten Defensive Player of the Year Shawn Springs did what?

14-20   Which stadium held the 100th meeting of "The Game" to be played between Ohio State and Michigan?

ANSWERS **GROUP 14**

14-1   Joe Germaine and Stanley Jackson, 1996

14-2   Woody Hayes, after beating Michigan 17-0 in 1955 for his second consecutive Big Ten Championship

14-3   Bill Jobko, 1954-55-56

14-4   Howard "Hopalong" Cassady, 1954 vs. Wisconsin (88 yards) and Ted Provost, 1968 vs. Purdue (35 yards)

14-5   Mike Nugent, 2004

14-6   Yassenoff Recruit Center

14-7   Four

14-8   29 tackles, Linebacker Chris Spielman, 1986

14-9   False: Joe Germaine (56), Bobby Hoying (57), and Troy Smith (54)

14-10   Seven. Karsatos, Tomczak, Frey, Germaine, Hoying, Schlichter, and Smith

14-11   Art Schlichter, 8,850 yards, 1978-1981

14-12   True: One player, Keith Byars, 2,448 yards, 1984 average 203.8 all-purpose yards per game

14-13   Bob Atha, Indiana 1981 and Mike Nugent, North Carolina State 2004

14-14   Tom Cousineau, 1978

14-15   1964, 583,740, seven games average 83,391

14-16   Matt Wilhelm

14-17   2-10-1

14-18   313 yards

14-19   "Slipped"

14-20   Michigan Stadium, November 22, 2003

QUESTIONS **GROUP 15** *Vintage*

15-1   Who kicked the "Fifth-Quarter" field goal to beat Illinois 29-26 in 1943?

15-2   When did the Ohio State goal posts get torn down for the first time?

15-3   Which head coach resigned because of "the tension brought about by the tremendous desire to win football games?"

15-4   Who was the best Big Ten team in the 1930s with back-to-back Big Ten Championships and also did not lose a home game for seven seasons?

15-5   The Big Ten Conference once denied Ohio State a Rose Bowl trip because of what?

15-6   The winning point margin of 292-6 was established by what team?

15-7   **T or F**   The great Buckeye Tradition of Gold Pants, Buckeye Grove, Captain's Breakfast and Block O all started in the 1930s during Francis Schmidt's term as Head Coach.

15-8   What year did Ohio State and Michigan play their first Big Ten Conference game?

15-9   Who was Ohio State's first, colorful, high-strutting, showman Drum Major?

15-10   When did the Ohio Stadium scholarship dorms start?

15-11   **T or F**   Ohio State beat The University of Chicago and the first Heisman Trophy winner Jay Berwanger in 1935.

15-12   Who was Ohio State's first, first round draft pick in professional football?

15-13   Which two consecutive years did a "vintage" Ohio State team win the Big Ten Title outright?

15-14   How many tries did it take for Ohio State to Beat Michigan for the first time?

15-15   "Hopalong" Cassady is known as the spark that started to make football at Ohio State "the way we know it today." Who was the spark to really get Ohio State football started in the beginning?

15-16   Illinois upset Ohio State in 1921, and came away with what nickname?

15-17   **T or F**   One of the "Four Horseman" from the famous Notre Dame backfield coached at Ohio State.

15-18   **T or F**   Michigan is the only Big Ten team to wear the famous "flying wing" helmet.

15-19   Who was the Big Ten head coach for 29 years that took his worst beating (40-0) from Ohio State?

15-20   Who was Ohio State's first opponent and in what year did they play?

ANSWERS GROUP 15 *Vintage*

15-1   Paul Stungis

15-2   1934 Michigan game, Ohio State winning 34-0

15-3   Wes Fesler 1947-1950, followed by Woody Hayes 1951-1978

15-4   Minnesota

15-5   1944, based on WWII travel regulations and restrictions

15-6   1917, with Chic Harley

15-7   True

15-8   1918

15-9   Edwin "Tubby" Essington 1920-1922

15-10 During the Great Depression to help students with housing, relocated in 2001

15-11 True: 20-13

15-12 Halfback James McDonald by the Philadelphia Eagles, 1938

15-13 1916-1917

15-14 16 tries, Buckeyes won 13-3 at Ann Arbor October 25, 1919

15-15 Chic Harley, recognized by Harley's Rock on High Street at Woodruff Avenue

15-16 "Fighting Illini"

15-17 True, Don Miller 29-32

15-18 False: several Big Ten schools did during the 1930s, including Ohio State

15-19 Bob Zuppke from Illinois, 1931

15-20 Ohio Wesleyan in 1890, Ohio State 20-Ohio Wesleyan 14

QUESTIONS **GROUP 16**

16-1 Since 1935, through 2006, how many times has "The Game" decided the Big Ten Champion?

16-2 Since 1935, through 2006, how many times has "The Game" had a direct affect determining the Big Ten Champion?

16-3 In 1998, how many games did quarterback Joe Germaine gain 300-plus yards in total offense?

16-4 In the 90s, Ohio State was the number one producer of NFL talent. How many players were taken in the first round of the NFL draft?

16-5 What is the title of the primary Ohio State fight song?

16-6 How many of Head Coach Woody Hayes' teams shut-out Michigan?

16-7 What year did Ohio State set records for rushing yards, attempts and touchdowns against Michigan?

16-8 Which Ohio State player has won "The Jim Thrope Award" for best defensive back?

16-9 Who came off the bench as a freshman, scored three touchdowns in his first game, and started every game thereafter?

16-10 Where is the College Football Hall of Fame museum located?

16-11 Who kicked the 34-yard winning field goal in the 1958 Rose Bowl (OSU vs. Oregon)?

16-12 How long was the winning streak of the Miami Hurricanes before the Buckeyes broke it in the 2002 National Championship Fiesta Bowl game?

16-13 What new tradition did Head Coach Jim Tressel start after every game...win or lose?

16-14 In 1985, a State of Ohio "House Resolution" named what song as Ohio's rock song?

16-15 The Big Ten Athlete of the Year is named for whom?

16-16 What are "The Silver Bullets?"

16-17 Who said the following? "Three things can happen when you pass, and two of them are bad."

16-18 Which Buckeye won the "Ray Guy Award" for being an outstanding punter?

16-19 What two years did Ohio State place eleven players on the All-Big Ten Team?

16-20 Which Heisman Trophy winning quarterback upset Ohio State in the 1971 Rose Bowl?

ANSWERS GROUP 16

16-1 21 times

16-2 23 times

16-3 Five

16-4 15 of Coach John Cooper's players

16-5 "Buckeye Battle Cry" is played when the band enters the stadium and after every touchdown

16-6 Three times. 1955, 1960 and 1962

16-7 1968, 421 yards, 79 attempts and seven touchdowns

16-8 Antoine Winfield, 1998

16-9 Howard "Hopalong" Cassady

16-10 111 South St. Joseph Street, South Bend, Indiana 46601. 1-800-440-3263

16-11 Don Sutherin, Ohio State 10-Oregon 7

16-12 34 games

16-13 The singing of "Carmen Ohio" in the End Zone to the Ohio State Marching Band

16-14 "Hang on Sloopy"

16-15 Started in 1982. Jesse Owens Athlete of the Year Award

16-16 The Ohio State Defensive Team

16-17 Woody Hayes

16-18 B.J. Sander, 2003

16-19 1969 and 1975

16-20 Jim Plunkett, Stanford 27-17

QUESTIONS **GROUP 17**

17-1 Who gained 400 yards in total offense in a single game for the Buckeyes?

17-2 Who holds the record for career all-purpose yards gained per game at Ohio State?

17-3 Who lead the nation in 2004 with five field goals over 50 yards long?

17-4 Who holds the record for solo tackles in a career at Ohio State?

17-5 Which year did Ohio State's total season attendance go over 1,000,000 fans?

17-6 Who said the following? "I don't know how I could ever have a win bigger than this one."

17-7 Which Ohio State head coach received a three-year contract extension on the same day he lost his fourth straight game to Michigan?

17-8 Being indoctrinated into the Ohio State Marching Band "Michigan Hate Club," you are told what quote?

17-9 Who is the only Ohio State player to start four consecutive Rose Bowls?

17-10 How many of Woody Hayes' players have been inducted into The College Football Hall of Fame?

17-11 Name Archie Griffin's two brothers that played at Ohio State.

17-12 Who is the only non-linebacker to have 200 solo tackles in his Buckeye career?

17-13 Who kicked three field goals and two extra points for the 1955 College All-Stars to upset the Cleveland Browns 30-27?

17-14 In what four-year period did Head Coach Wood Hayes win three Big Ten Titles and two National Championships?

17-15 Kicking more field goals was encouraged starting in what season, by widening the goal post to 24 feet?

17-16 What was Head Coach Woody Hayes record against Northwestern coach Ara Parseghian before Ara moved on to Notre Dame?

17-17 Notre Dame returned to Columbus in 1995 after 60 years absence since "The Game of the Century" to what result?

17-18 Which player on the 2002 National Championship team played offense, defense, and special teams?

17-19 When Jim Tressel breaks this coaches' record, who was the coach who had been the second most-winning head coach at Ohio State?

17-20 **T or F** From 1972 to 1977, Woody Hayes' teams won or shared six Big Ten Titles.

ANSWERS GROUP 17

17-1   Art Schlichter, 1981
17-2   Archie Griffin, 145.8 yards per game, 6,558 yards, 1972-1975
17-3   Mike Nugent
17-4   Chris Spielman, 283 solo tackles, 1984-1987
17-5   1975
17-6   Lloyd Carr, rookie head-coaching year at Michigan in 1995, remember "Bo" in 1968?
17-7   John Cooper
17-8   "Michigan is north until you smell it and west until you step in it."
17-9   Archie Griffin
17-10   11
17-11   Duncan and Ray Griffin
17-12   Antoine Winfield
17-13   Tad Weed
17-14   1954 through 1957
17-15   1959
17-16   1 - 3
17-17   Notre Dame losing 45 to 26
17-18   Chris Gamble
17-19   Head Coach John Cooper
17-20   True: five ties, one outright in 1975

QUESTIONS GROUP 18

18-1 What team posted the first-ever Division 1A record of 14-0?

18-2 How many ties have the Ohio State Buckeyes and Michigan Wolverines had?

18-3 What was Woody's greatest offensive showing in a bowl game?

18-4 Head Coach John Cooper led his Buckeyes to 11 bowl games during his tenure. How many did he win?

18-5 In nine seasons, what was Head Coach Earle Bruce's record?

18-6 Name two Ohio State football players that made the "Wheaties" box cover.

18-7 Who won the first Buckeye Leaf Award (sticker) for outstanding play?

18-8 Name the six Ohio State Heisman Trophy Award winners.

18-9 Which 1950 alumnus and comic strip artist drew the original design of the Ohio State Buckeye Leaf?

18-10 Which kicker hit five 50-yard field goals in his career and tied a record of five field goals in one game during a single season?

18-11 Which two buildings (structures) greatly influenced the design of The Ohio Stadium?

18-12 What was the title of the most successful song The Beatles ever released when the Buckeyes were also No. 1 in 1968?

18-13 The house that "The Babe" built was Yankee Stadium. Who caused The Ohio Stadium "house" to be built?

18-14 Which running back holds the records for the most yards in a single game (314), and the most yards in a single season (1,927)?

18-15 TBDBITL is an acronym for what?

18-16 What year did Brutus Buckeye first appear?

18-17 Where is the James Cleveland Memorial statue?

18-18 What year celebrated the 125th year of college football, which started with Rutgers vs. Princeton?

18-19 **T or F** Woody Hayes, Ara Parseghian, and Bo Schembechler all coached at "The Cradle of Coaches."

18-20 Head Coach Earle Bruce was a head coach at what two colleges before he came to Ohio State in 1979?

ANSWERS GROUP 18

18-1   2002 Ohio State National Champion Buckeyes

18-2   Six. 1900, 1910, 1941, 1949, 1973, and 1992

18-3   1975 Rose Bowl, Ohio State 42-USC 21

18-4   Three

18-5   81-26-1

18-6   Tom Matte and Chris Spielman

18-7   Jim Nein (#9), 1967

18-8   Les Horvath (1944), Vic Janowicz (1950), "Hopalong" Cassady (1955), Archie Griffin (1974-1975), Eddie George (1995), and Troy Smith (2006)

18-9   Milton Caniff

18-10 Two-time All-American Kicker Mike Nugent

18-11 Pantheon and Roman Coliseum

18-12 "Hey Jude"

18-13 "Chic" Harley

18-14 Eddie George, 1995 Heisman Trophy winner

18-15 "The Best Damn Band in the Land"

18-16 1965

18-17 The James Cleveland (Jesse Owens) Memorial is located outside Ohio Stadium at the north entrance.

18-18 1994

18-19 True: Miami University of Ohio

18-20 University of Tampa and Iowa State University

QUESTIONS GROUP 19

19-1 During "Michigan Week," what is the big ritual that students partake in on Thursday night?

19-2 Composer John Philip Sousa called what song "college's best fight song?"

19-3 The Outland Trophy and the Vince Lombardi Award for honoring lineman has been won twice by which two Ohio State players?

19-4 Who was the nickel back that intercepted UM's John Navarre's pass to Braylon Edwards to insure victory (14 to 9) in 2002 and a trip to the Fiesta Bowl National Championship Game?

19-5 How many three-time All-Americans did Head Coach Wood Hayes have play for him?

19-6 Which Buckeye won the Dave Rimmington Trophy for the Outstanding Center in 2001?

19-7 **T or F** Woody Hayes had at least one All-Big Ten Player every year for twenty-eight years.

19-8 What year (season) was the two-point extra point option added after a touchdown?

19-9 Which Ohio State quarterback had the most pass completions in a single season?

19-10 Which head coach had a better winning percentage, Earle Bruce or John Cooper?

19-11 Which Ohio State lineman finished second in the Heisman Trophy voting in 1973?

19-12 Which OSU QB made his first start at UM and won the game for the first time in Ann Arbor since 1987?

19-13 What year did only three Ohio State players get drafted into the NFL, but all three went to the same team, the Cleveland Browns?

19-14 In which bowl game has Ohio State had their most touchdown passes?

19-15 John Cooper's 100th victory came with one second left on the clock, with a pass reception by whom?

19-16 Who holds the record for the most rushing yards per game for a single season at Ohio State and who holds the record for the most rushing yards for a career?

19-17 Who holds the Ohio State record for most pass receptions in a single game?

19-18 Who punted for over 5½ miles in yards during his career at Ohio State?

19-19 Which two athletic facilities were named after the two gentlemen most responsible for the construction of the Ohio Stadium?

19-20 In which game did Ohio State stop their opponent on the six-inch yard line, then drive the distance of the field to score the winning touchdown?

ANSWERS GROUP 19

19-1 Jumping into Mirror Lake

19-2 "The Victors," The University of Michigan

19-3 John Hicks (1973) and Orlando Pace (1996)

19-4 Will Allen

19-5 Two. Archie Griffin and Tom Skladany

19-6 Le Charles Bentley

19-7 True

19-8 1958

19-9 Joe Germaine, 230, 1998

19-10 Earle Bruce .755 vs. .702

19-11 John Hicks, 1973 to Jon Cappelletti of Penn State

19-12 Craig Krenzel, 2001

19-13 1960. Jim Marshall, Jim Houston, and Bob White

19-14 Four. 2004 Fiesta Bowl vs. Kansas State

19-15 Bobby Olive

19-16 Eddie George (148.2) 1995 and Archie Griffin (117.3) 1972-1975

19-17 David Boston. 14 vs. Penn State 1997

19-18 Brent Bartholomew, 9,927 yards, 1995-1998

19-19 St. John Arena (L.W. St. John AD) and French Field House (Professor Thomas E. French)

19-20 Michigan game 1954, 21-7

QUESTIONS GROUP 20 *Vintage*

20-1 Who is the only head coach in Ohio State history to start 2-0 against Michigan before 1950?

20-2 WBNS-TV in Columbus, Ohio aired the first coach's show in the country. Who was the coach?

20-3 Which All-American served in World War I (1918)?

20-4 What was the contract price for the construction of The Ohio Stadium in 1921?

20-5 Who was the architect for The Ohio Stadium project?

20-6 Who holds the record for the longest kick-off return of 103 yards for Ohio State?

20-7 Who is the only head coach to shut-out Michigan four years in a row?

20-8 Name the three NFL Hall of Fame players on the original Cleveland Browns team in 1947 that played at Ohio State.

20-9 He was a two-time All-American at end (1932-33), coached 21 years in college, head coach of NFL Los Angeles Rams and AFL San Diego Chargers winning division titles. Who is he?

20-10 Why did Michigan coach Fritz Crisler introduce the "yellow wing" helmet in the 1930s?

20-11 Who holds the record for the most punt attempts in a single game?

20-12 Which Michigan player gave the greatest performance in an Ohio State game when he was 11 for 12 in passing for 151 yards and two touchdowns, ran for 139 yards and two touchdowns, intercepted three passes, kicked four extra points and averaged 50 yards per punt?

20-13 Which famous Michigan coach pronounced Michigan with his southern drawl as "Meechigan?"

20-14 **T or F** James Thurber, OSU grad, humorist, writer, and artist never designed an Ohio State football program.

20-15 What year was the Ohio State vs. Michigan game moved to the final week of conference play?

20-16 Who was the great innovator, credited with the idea for the Super Bowl, the AFC-NFL World Championship?

20-17 He played with "Chic" Harley, then coached the Columbus Tigers pro team in 1922. Who was he?

20-18 Before they played in The Big Ten Conference, what conference did Ohio State play in?

20-19 Which team in 1935 scored three touchdowns in the 4th quarter to overcome a 13-0 score to win 18-13?

20-20 Who was the first Ohio State player to be All-Big Ten in three consecutive seasons?

ANSWERS GROUP 20 *Vintage*

20-1 Head Coach Francis Schmidt, in fact he went 4 - 0 1934-1937
20-2 Head Coach Wes Fesler, 1948
20-3 "Chic" Harley
20-4 $1,341,017.00 to E.H. Latham Co., Columbus, Ohio. Final cost $1,488,168.00
20-5 Howard Dwight Smith, won the gold medal from AIA for "Excellence in Public Work"
20-6 Dean Sensanbaugher, 1943
20-7 Francis Schmidt 1934-35-36-37
20-8 Lou Groza, Dante Lavelli, and Bill Willis
20-9 Sid Gillman
20-10 So the quarterback could distinguish his receivers in the early days of the "forward pass"
20-11 Vic Janowicz, 21, Michigan 1950
20-12 Tom Harmon, 1940, Two-time All-American, Heisman Trophy Award Winner
20-13 Head Coach Fielding Yost
20-14 False: Ohio State vs. Michigan, November 21, 1936 (Homecoming). Only cover he did.
20-15 1935
20-16 Sid Gillman
20-17 All-American Pete Stinchcomb
20-18 Western Conference
20-19 Notre Dame
20-20 Wes Fesler 1928-29-30 and "Chic" Harley did it 1916-17 and 1919

QUESTIONS GROUP 21

21-1   Which Ohio State running back won the Doak Walker Award, Maxwell Award, Walter Camp Player of the Year, and Heisman Trophy in one year?

21-2   Which Buckeye football players have won the Big Ten Athlete of the Year Award?

21-3   Who caught the winning touchdown pass from Joe Germaine in the 1997 Rose Bowl?

21-4   What former Ohio State quarterback became a Major League Baseball pitcher?

21-5   What is Ohio State's record for bowl games from 1920 through 2006?

21-6   **T or F**   Woody Hayes won eight out of ten Michigan games from 1954 until 1964.

21-7   What team won a Big Ten Title in 1995 and shared one in 1996 when they did not play Ohio State?

21-8   What were the most points scored by the Buckeyes in a bowl game?

21-9   Name the father and son who both had key interceptions in the "Horseshoe."

21-10 Who holds the season and career records for the most rushing touchdowns?

21-11 What is the latest example of the Heisman jinx?

21-12 Ernie Godfrey, a National Football Foundation Hall of Fame member, coached how many years at Ohio State?

21-13 What is the greatest comeback victory in Ohio State history?

21-14 Through 2006, what is Ohio State's all-time record when they were No. 1?

21-15 How many 9-3 seasons in a row did Head Coach Earle Bruce have at Ohio State?

21-16 **T or F**   Head Coaches Woody Hayes and John Cooper both had five seasons with ten or more victories.

21-17 How many 200-yard rushing games did Archie Griffin have in his Ohio State career?

21-18 In 1969, fullback Jim Otis became the first 1,000-yard running back. How many has Ohio State had since?

21-19 What year was Woody Hayes' Ohio State team put on probation for "irregularities?"

21-20 The 1975 win at Michigan (21-14) stopped Michigan's consecutive home win record at what number?

ANSWERS GROUP 21

21-1   Eddie George, 1995
21-2   Eddie George, 1996 and Troy Smith, 2006
21-3   David Boston
21-4   Joe Sparma
21-5   18 - 20
21-6   True: only loss in 1956 and 1959
21-7   Northwestern
21-8   47 points vs. BYU in 1982 Holiday Bowl
21-9   Howard "Hopalong" Cassady and his son Craig Cassady
21-10 Pete Johnson (25), 1975 and career (56) 1973-1976
21-11 2007 BCS Championship Game
21-12 33 years
21-13 31-0 deficit to win 41-37 at Minnesota, 1989
21-14 63-9-1
21-15 Six. 1980-1985
21-16 True: although most of Woody Hayes' seasons were nine games and John Cooper's were 12 games.
21-17 Two. 239 yards first game, 246 yards vs. Iowa 1973
21-18 23 total, including Jim Otis
21-19 1956
21-20 41

QUESTIONS GROUP 22

22-1 One of Columbus' most famous addresses is Woody Hayes' home. What is the address?

22-2 Lame duck Head Coach Earle Bruce was supported by his players in his final game against Michigan in 1987 by displaying what?

22-3 Which Ohio State freshman tied the NCAA record with four punt returns for touchdowns?

22-4 Who said the following? "I am not trying to win a popularity poll; I'm trying to win football games."

22-5 Which Ohio State team defeated three top five teams, Notre Dame No. 4, Penn State No. 3, and Arizona State No. 2, and finished No. 2 in the national polls?

22-6 What rank in the United States Navy during WWII did Head Coach Woody Hayes achieve?

22-7 Who holds the record for the most rushing yards in a single season at Ohio State?

22-8 Who has the record for the most solo tackles in a career at Ohio State?

22-9 Who was the hero of the 2002 Penn State game with a touchdown, saving tackle from behind, and an interception for a touchdown that helped to send the Buckeyes to the National Championship Game?

22-10 Which kicker won three games with last minute field goals in a single season?

22-11 Which Columbus restaurant used Woody's picture and the ad line "In All the World There's Only One?"

22-12 Who scored twice on 88-yard runs, one from scrimmage and one a kick-off return in a single game?

22-13 **T or F** Since 1951 Ohio State has won three out of four ball games under Hayes, Bruce, Cooper, and Tressel.

22-14 Who was the first receiver to gain over 1,000 yards in a season at Ohio State?

22-15 What did "So they wouldn't storm the castle" mean?

22-16 What three years did the Michigan State Spartans upset Ohio State and destroy their National Championship goals?

22-17 What was the worst "homer" call against Woody Hayes' Buckeyes, which resulted in a 15-yard penalty for "unsportsmanlike conduct" for Woody?

22-18 Who said the following? "Bulletin board material? All Ohio football players don't go to Michigan, only the good ones."

22-19 Who blocked Iowa's Greg Kostrubali's punt for a safety when Ohio State upset No. 1 Iowa in 1985?

22-20 How many points did Ohio State score in the fourth quarter when they beat Michigan 50-20 in 1961?

ANSWERS **GROUP 22**

22-1   1711 Cardiff Road, Upper Arlington, Ohio 43220

22-2   "EARLE" Headbands

22-3   Ted Ginn Jr., 2004

22-4   Woody Hayes

22-5   1996 Team

22-6   Lt. Commander

22-7   Eddie George, 1,927 yards, 1995

22-8   Chris Spielman, 283, 1984 –1987

22-9   Chris Gamble

22-10 Bob Funk, 1965, 23 -21 vs. Wisconsin, 11-10 Minnesota, and 9 -7 over Michigan

22-11 Jai Lai, now the Buckeye Hall of Fame

22-12 Morris Bradshaw vs. Wisconsin, 1971

22-13 True: actually a little better than 75%

22-14 Chris Carter, 1986, 1,127 yards on 69 receptions

22-15 Woody Hayes would punt on third down, so the opponents would not rush nine men on fourth down

22-16 1972, 1974, and 1998

22-17 1971. Michigan's Darden over the back pass interference on Ohio State's Dick Wakefield

22-18 Michigan's quarterback Dennis Franklin, 1972. Oh, Michigan lost that game!

22-19 Sonny Gordon

22-20 29 points

QUESTIONS GROUP 23

23-1 How many times during the Ohio State vs. Michigan rivalry have both teams had a losing season?

23-2 Who is the career leader in "sacks" for the Buckeyes?

23-3 **T or F** One time only has Ohio State lost four consecutive bowl games.

23-4 Which Ohio State quarterback had the most yards passing in a season and in a career?

23-5 Who said the following? "Help young people as someone helped you when you were young. Invest in the future."

23-6 Who were the "men of brutality?"

23-7 What was Penn State's first year in the Big Ten Conference, making it 11 teams?

23-8 How many No. 1 teams did Head Coach Earle Bruce defeat?

23-9 Linebacker Jim Laughlin blocked the punt; who ran it in from 18 yards out for the winning touchdown at Michigan 1979?

23-10 Howard "Hopalong" Cassady was what team's worst nightmare?

23-11 The 235-member Michigan Marching Band has what for its trademark formation?

23-12 What "Super Sophomore" was the MVP of the 1969 Rose Bowl Game?

23-13 Who carried the ball 11 of 14 plays in an 80-yard drive to beat Big Ten Champion Iowa 38-28 in 1958?

23-14 Name the leading pass catcher with four receptions for 50 yards in 1955.

23-15 Who is the single season and career kickoff returner at Ohio State?

23-16 **T or F** Chris Carter caught more passes in 1986 than any of Woody Hayes' leading receivers totaled together from 1954 through 1960.

23-17 Which Ohio State linebacker had over 200 total tackles in a season?

23-18 Which Ohio State defensive back twice had three interceptions in a game?

23-19 What is the longest passing play in Ohio State history?

23-20 How many "National Coach of the Year" Awards did Head Coach Woody Hayes win?

ANSWERS GROUP 23

23-1   Once in 1959, Ohio State 3-5-1, Michigan 4-5

23-2   Mike Vrabel (36), 1993-1996

23-3   False: Woody Hayes' last two and Earle Bruce's first two; John Cooper's 1990-1993 teams

23-4   Joe Germaine 3,330 yards, 1998 and Art Schlichter 7,547 yards, 1978-1981

23-5   Woody Hayes. "You can never pay back, but you can always pay forward."

23-6   Defensive backs for Head Coach Earle Bruce

23-7   1993

23-8   One. Iowa 1985, 22-13

23-9   Todd Bell... then on to the Rose Bowl as Big Ten Champions

23-10   Wisconsin... always a Buckeye Victory

23-11   A big capital block "M"

23-12   Quarterback Rex Kern

23-13   Fullback Bob White, overall 209 yards rushing, three touchdowns

23-14   Bill Michael

23-15   Ken-Yon Rambo 1997-2000

23-16   True: 69 vs. 67

23-17   Chris Spielman, 205, 1986 and Tom Cousineau, 244, 1978

23-18   Fred Bruney, Illinois 1951 and Michigan 1952, 17 total interceptions in his career

23-19   Art Schlichter to Calvin Murray, 86 yards vs. Washington State, 1979

23-20   Three. 1957, 1968 and 1975

QUESTIONS **GROUP 24**

24-1 Name the three running backs in Woody Hayes T-formation for the 1961 National Champions.

24-2 Two "Goal Line Stands" by the underdog Buckeyes proved to be the deciding factor in beating Michigan in what year?

24-3 **T or F** When Woody Hayes teams were ranked No. 1 he was upset only five times.

24-4 Which team has Ohio State beaten the most over the years?

24-5 **T or F** All the scoring in the "Snow Bowl" came from blocked punts.

24-6 What is the number one selling item for "Fan Spirit" at Ohio State?

24-7 Who is the career punt return yardage leader?

24-8 Who has caught the most passes for Ohio State in a single game?

24-9 Which Ohio State kickoff returner has the most yards in a single game?

24-10 Marcus Marek is first in career total tackles at 572, who is second and third?

24-11 Which season did three Buckeyes finish in the top six voting for the Heisman Trophy won by John Cappelletti of Penn State?

24-12 **T or F** Art Schlichter was never a finalist in the Heisman Trophy voting.

24-13 What was the first year that Ohio State averaged over 80,000 fans, 90,000 fans and 100,000 fans in home attendance?

24-14 What two major football programs from southern schools both have a 3-0 record against the Buckeyes?

24-15 Which former Ohio State player and coach, unranked, upset the fifth ranked Ohio State Buckeyes in "The Horseshoe" in 2000?

24-16 Through 2006, what was the last home opener lost by the Buckeyes?

24-17 Who was the first Ohio State quarterback to throw for 300 yards in two consecutive games?

24-18 Who is the only coach from the Big Ten and the Pac-10 to win a Rose Bowl?

24-19 In what football game do all the proceeds go to The Black Coaches Association?

24-20 Who said the following? "I think that was the finest individual effort I've ever seen by a running back."

ANSWERS GROUP 24

24-1   Paul Warfield, Bob Ferguson, and Matt Snell

24-2   1972

24-3   True: four loses and a 10-10 tie at Michigan in 1973

24-4   Indiana, followed by Illinois and Northwestern

24-5   False: all of Michigan's points did, Ohio State's Vic Janowicz kicked a field goal. Final score Michigan 9-Ohio State 3

24-6   Black baseball cap with Scarlet Block "O", aka "Woody's Hat"

24-7   Ted Ginn Jr.

24-8   David Boston, 14, 1997 vs. Penn State

24-9   Carlos Snow, 213 yards vs. Pittsburgh, 1988

24-10   Tom Cousineau, 569; Chris Spielman 546

24-11   1973: John Hicks 2nd, Archie Griffin 5th and Randy Gradishar 6th

24-12   False: he was 4th 1979, 5th 1981 and 6th in 1980

24-13   1954: 80,000, 1988 90,000 and 2001 100,000

24-14   Florida State and Alabama

24-15   Glen Mason, Minnesota 29-17

24-16   Penn State 19-0, 1978

24-17   Joe Germaine, Illinois, and Minnesota 1998

24-18   Head Coach John Cooper

24-19   Eddie Robinson Football Classic

24-20   John Cooper, about Eddie George's 314 rushing yards against Illinois

QUESTIONS GROUP 25 *Vintage*

25-1 **T or F** Red Grange (Illinois) and Tom Harmon (Michigan), both Heisman Trophy winners, played their last college game in "The Horseshoe."

25-2 During the seasons from 1902 to 1921, which conference did Ohio State play in?

25-3 Who holds the Ohio State record for the most yards punting in a game?

25-4 What is Ohio State's all-time record against Notre Dame?

25-5 "The Perfect Play" was what?

25-6 What year did Ohio State win its first Rose Bowl and who did they defeat?

25-7 During the seasons from 1916 to 1949, how many Big Ten Championships and Co-Championships did Ohio State win?

25-8 Who was Ohio State's first African-American All-American (actually two-time) and first African-American to start for the Pros?

25-9 Which player and former assistant coach has the most pairs of "Gold Pants?"

25-10 How many outright Big Ten Titles did Ohio State win in the "vintage" years?

25-11 What famous coach had an agreement to coach at Ohio State in 1929, but was convinced to stay where he had a contract already in place?

25-12 Who was the first head coach to have a coaching contract longer than a year?

25-13 The rule: "A player could not return in any quarter after being taken out in that same quarter" affected what famous game?

25-14 **T or F** Ara Parseghian played for Head Coach Paul Brown while at Ohio State.

25-15 What head coach in his first year, was coach of the Associated Press No. 2 team, but the "National Civilian Champions?"

25-16 What is a "Grid-Graf?"

25-17 How many of the Kabealo brothers played at Ohio State?

25-18 My dad was an ATO, but he was also a member of the non-fraternity fraternity in the 30s at Smitty's Drugstore at 16th and High Streets. What was this organization's name?

25-19 What Big Ten team was the first Associated Press Mythical National Champion in 1936?

25-20 What period of time was Ohio State called the "Graveyard of Coaches?"

ANSWERS GROUP 25 *Vintage*

25-1 True

25-2 Ohio Athletic Conference

25-3 Vic Janowicz, 685 yards, 1950 "Snow Bowl" vs. Michigan

25-4 3-2

25-5 End-around running play, that went for three touchdowns in Ohio State's win against Northwestern, 1916.

25-6 January 2, 1950, Ohio State beat California 17-14

25-7 Six Championships; two Co-Championships

25-8 Bill Willis

25-9 Esco Sarkkinen

25-10 Six

25-11 Knute Rockne

25-12 Head Coach Francis Schmidt, three years 1934-35-36

25-13 Notre Dame 1935, "Game of the Century"

25-14 False: Ara Parseghian played fullback for Paul Brown at the Great Lakes Naval Training Center "Blue Jackets" vs. Ohio State in 1944

25-15 Head Coach Carroll Widdoes, 1944

25-16 A line drawing depicting all the plays on a football field template

25-17 Four

25-18 Si U.

25-19 Minnesota

25-20 1944-1950

QUESTIONS **GROUP 26**

26-1 Who is the only barber to cut the hair of head coaches Hayes, Bruce, Cooper, and Tressel?

26-2 How many passes did Troy Smith throw in his freshman year?

26-3 Who said "November is for contenders?"

26-4 Who holds the Big Ten single-season record for interceptions?

26-5 Who was the "Butkus Award" winner that scored a touchdown on a blocked punt in his last home game in 2005?

26-6 Name the five former Ohio State head coaches who have been inducted into the College Football Hall of Fame.

26-7 When was the last year "The Game" was not a sell-out?

26-8 Who was the honoree in 2006 to dot the "i"?

26-9 Besides Ohio State, what other school has won seven Heisman Trophies?

26-10 Who was the 1985 favorite to win the Heisman trophy, but a broken foot caused him to miss most of the season?

26-11 Michigan State upset the #1 Buckeyes 28-24 in 1998. How many points underdog were they?

26-12 Before the 2007 BCS Championship Game, OSU vs. Florida, how many times before had they met?

26-13 In the 1960s, which of the Ohio State vs. Michigan games was delayed for a week?

26-14 How many times have Ohio State vs. Michigan been ranked #1 vs. #2?

26-15 What is the Buckeyes favorite fast food restaurant in Scottsdale, Arizona during bowl games?

26-16 Who was the first Buckeye to win the Thorpe Award as the country's outstanding defensive back?

26-17 How many NFL Hall of Fame members from Ohio State have played for the Cleveland Browns?

26-18 Who was *Columbus Monthly* magazine's 2006 Person of the Year?

26-19 After the 2006 Michigan game, who still holds the record for most yards rushing?

26-20 What player from Columbus West High School was 1st Team All-American, won a Big Ten Championship, National Title, and the Rose Bowl?

ANSWERS GROUP 26

26-1 Howard Warner, Howard's Barber Shop

26-2 Zero, Troy was a kick return player and backup running back

26-3 Head coach Earle Bruce

26-4 Craig Cassady, 9 interceptions, 1975 "Hops" son

26-5 A. J. Hawk #47

26-6 Howard Jones, John Wilce, Francis Schmidt, Woody Hayes and Earle Bruce

26-7 1967

26-8 Jack Nicklaus, all-time golf great.
Minnesota Game October 28, 2006

26-9 (2) Southern California (USC), Norte Dame (ND)

26-10 RB Keith Byers

26-11 28 point underdog

26-12 Never, this was their first game.

26-13 1963, because of the JFK assassination

26-14 One time, 2006

26-15 IN and OUT Burger

26-16 Antoine Winfield

26-17 (4) Bill Willis, Lou Groza, Dante Lavelli and Paul Warfield, (1) coach Paul Brown

26-18 QB Troy Smith

26-19 Dave Francis, 1962, 31 carries, 186 yards

26-20 Aurealius Thomas

QUESTIONS **GROUP 27**

27-1   Who was the All-American end in 1958 who also held the school record in discus and shot-put?

27-2   Varsity "O" President Waldo and which Athletic Director started the Athletics Hall of Fame at OSU?

27-3   What was the winning Pick-4 number in Ohio's Lottery November 18, 2006?

27-4   How many players were drafted in the first round of the 2006 NFL draft? Name them.

27-5   What year was Ohio State ranked #1 in football and basketball?

27-6   What two Big Ten schools have won an NCAA National Championship in football, basketball and baseball?

27-7   Who was the MVP for the 2006 Big Ten Champions, Ohio State Buckeyes?

27-8   Who was drafted (1 of 11) in 1976 before two-time Heisman Trophy winner Archie Griffin?

27-9   Who set the Ohio State record for receptions by a running back with 47 catches?

27-10   Who was known as "Wagon?"

27-11   The acronym TSUN stands for what?

27-12   **T or F**   Ohio State plays in front of a million "fans in the stands" annually?

27-13   What two players were on the cover of the 2007 BCS National Championship Game program?

27-14   What years was Jim Tressel an assistant coach at Ohio State under head coach Earle Bruce?

27-15   How many days were there between the 2006 OSU-Michigan game and the BCS Championship game?

27-16   **T or F**   The underdog has won straight up, not just covering the Vegas spread, 6 of the last 8 BCS Championship games through 2006-07 season.

27-17   Who was the second Ohio State QB to BEAT MICHIGAN three times in a row?

27-18   Name the running backs who have put together back-to-back 1,000-yard rushing seasons?

27-19   Who was the Buckeye "Fun Bunch?"

27-20   What National award did sophomore All-American LB James Laurinaitis win in 2006?

ANSWERS GROUP 27

27-1 Jim Marshall

27-2 AD Ed Weaver, first class 1977

27-3 4239. Same as the score OSU 42, Michigan 39 STRANGE!

27-4 5 AJ Hawk, Dante Whitner, Bobby Carpenter, Santonio Holmes, and Nick Mangold

27-5 2006, 11/27/2006

27-6 The Ohio State University and the University of Michigan

27-7 QB Troy Smith #10

27-8 DB Tim Fox

27-9 RB Eddie George 1995

27-10 MLB Jim Stillwagon, two-time All-American

27-11 "That School Up North"

27-12 True

27-13 Troy Smith #10 Ohio State; Chris Leak #12 Florida

27-14 1984-85

27-15 51 days—a long time to sit out!

27-16 True

27-17 QB Troy Smith #10; 2004-05-06

27-18 Archie Griffin (73-74-75), Tim Spencer (81-82), Keith Byers (83-84), Eddie George (94-95), Antonio Pittman (05-06)

27-19 QB Troy Smith, WR Ted Ginn Jr., WR Anthony Gonzalezand, TB Antonio Pittman

27-20 Bronko Nagurski award and he was a finalist for the Butkus Award

QUESTIONS GROUP 28

28-1 Who was the first Buckeye linebacker to earn All-American honors?

28-2 Which Big Ten team has the "White Wave" student body cheering section?

28-3 Who was Ohio State's 7th winner of the Heisman trophy?

28-4 What sports agency called the Ohio State Michigan football game the greatest rivalry in sports?

28-5 Who was signed first and last in the 2002 recruiting class?

28-6 Name the seven years the Ohio State Buckeyes have won National Championships in football.

28-7 Before 2006, when was the last time Ohio State and Michigan met as unbeatens?

28-8 What great Ohio State tradition do most men "tear-up?"

28-9 What is the title of the book about "The life and times of Woody Hayes" by John Lombardo?

28-10 Where did former head coach Earle Bruce coach after being fired by Ohio State?

28-11 From 1914 (Boyd Cherry) to 2005 (A J Hawk) how many 1st team All-Americans have been honored in the "Buckeye Grove?"

28-12 The 1942 National Champs received their rings from whom?

28-13 Troy Smith out-paced the second place finisher in the Heisman trophy by how many points?

28-14 The *Daily Oklahoman* newspaper called Ohio State the number one school for what on July 10, 2006?

28-15 What was the final score of the 2007 BCS National Championship game against Florida?

28-16 Who played for Woody at Miami University (49-50) and later coached at Yale for 32 seasons?

28-17 Name the two All-Americans who played for Bob Stuart at Eastmoor High School in Columbus.

28-18 Who ran the opening 2007 BCS National Championship kick-off back for a touchdown?

28-19 Which deck in Ohio Stadium has the most seats?

28-20 The Wuerffel trophy for exemplary community service with athletic and academic achievement was won by which Buckeye in 2006?

ANSWERS GROUP 28

28-1   Dwight "Ike" Kelly

28-2   Penn State: A "tough" stadium to visit and play in.

28-3   QB Troy Smith #10, 2006

28-4   ESPN-ABC

28-5   Maurice Clarett (first), Troy Smith (last)

28-6   1942 Paul Brown; 1954, 1957, 1961, 1968, 1970 Woody Hayes; 2002 Jim Tressel

28-7   1973

28-8   The "RAMP" entrance of TBDBITL

28-9   *A Fire to Win*

28-10 University of Northern Iowa and Colorado State

28-11 125

28-12 Coach Jim Tressel because he read they had never gotten their rings because of WWII. He awarded them in 2002 along with his National Championship team.

28-13 1662 points

28-14 Running backs

28-15 Florida 41, Ohio State 14

28-16 Coach Carmen Cozza

28-17 Doug Van Horn and Archie Griffin

28-18 WR Ted Ginn Jr.

28-19 30,878 "C" Deck

28-20 Joel Penton

QUESTIONS GROUP 29

29-1 Who was Ohio State's first All-American defensive back?

29-2 Who was Ohio State's first 1000-yard rusher?

29-3 Who kicked a record 54-yard field goal against Illinois in 1975?

29-4 Which Heisman trophy winner scored three touchdowns in his first game at Ohio State?

29-5 Who was the net 1000-yard rusher after freshman Maurice Clarett?

29-6 Which coach taught passionately "that a person succeeds in life through 'outworking' the opposition?"

29-7 Which professional team took two Buckeyes in the 2006 NFL draft?

29-8 Going into "The Game" 2006, what was the series record for the last 50 years?

29-9 Before 2006, had Ohio State and Michigan ever met as #1 vs. #2?

29-10 When was the first year they planted buckeye trees in the "Buckeye Grove?"

29-11 Name the two defensive backs that intercepted passes against Penn State and returned them for touchdowns in 2006.

29-12 Who won the Archie Griffin Award for Outstanding Offensive Player in 2006?

29-13 What state has the most native sons as Heisman trophy winners?

29-14 Who won the Lombardi Award and Outland Trophy in 1996?

29-15 How many unbeaten seasons have been destroyed in the past Ohio State-Michigan games?

29-16 The Ohio State marching band performed what sinking formation at the 2007 BCS game?

29-17 **T or F** The last three games in the University of Phoenix Stadium 06/07 where won by teams wearing blue and orange.

29-18 **T or F** Did the total attendance of NCAA football games in 2006 set a new record?

29-19 **T or F** Super Bowl Chicago Bears head coach Louie Smith coached at Ohio State.

29-20 What was the date when Wayne Woodrow Hayes passed away?

ANSWERS GROUP 29

29-1   Arnold Chonko

29-2   FB Jim Otis, 1969, 1027 yards, 219 carries

29-3   Tom Skladany, 1975

29-4   RB Howard "Hopalong" Cassady #40, vs. Indiana 1952

29-5   RB Antonio Pittman #25, 2005-06

29-6   Head Coach Wayne Woodrow "Woody" Hayes

29-7   New York Jets, Nick Mangold and Anthony Schlegel

29-8   24-24-2

29-9   NO!

29-10 1934

29-11 Malcolm Jenkins 61 yards, Antonio Smith 55 yards

29-12 Ted Ginn Jr.

29-13 The Great State of OHIO

29-14 Orlando Pace

29-15 10

29-16 Titanic

29-17 True: Boise State (Oklahoma), Denver Broncos (Cardinals) and Florida Gators (Ohio State)… all losing teams wearing red.

29-18 True: nearly 48 million fans

29-19 True: 1995 assistant coach to John Cooper

29-20 March 12, 1987

QUESTIONS GROUP 30

30-1 What two football coaches and three Heisman Trophy winners were inducted into the first class of the Varsity "O" Hall of Fame?

30-2 Which player was a two-time All American guard, Team Captain (1946) and played guard on the 1946 Big Ten Basketball Championship team?

30-3 What is Ohio State's worst defeat in the modern era?

30-4 Who was the first quarterback to Beat Michigan three times in a row?

30-5 Which Buckeye was one of the original four to first break the color line in the NFL?

30-6 Who came back with an "extra year" ruling because of WWII to win the Heisman Trophy?

30-7 When was the first year Ohio State was ranked in the Top 10 by a wire service?

30-8 How many points did Alabama score against the Bucks in the first half of the 1977 Sugar Bowl?

30-9 What is the Dunkel?

30-10 **T or F** Mickey Vuchinich kicked a winning field goal 32 ft. and winning extra point of 33 ft., OSU vs. Illinois, to win a National Championship in '33.

30-11 Which Ohio State QB holds the record for single season touchdown passes at 30?

30-12 Who invented the WEED tennis racket?

30-13 **T or F** Jim Parker held Michigan to 8 ft. on four running plays to stop them on the 1-yard line.

30-14 How many yards and which game did QB Troy Smith set career marks for most passing yards?

30-15 Name the three Number 2 ranked teams Ohio State played in 2006.

30-16 **T or F** QB Troy Smith was not the first Big Ten or Ohio State QB to win the Heisman Trophy.

30-17 Who is the Ohio State career leader in punt returns for touchdowns, with 6?

30-18 What do these National Champion football coaches have in common; Carroll (USC), Coker (Miami), Saban (LSU), Holtz (ND) and Tressel (OSU)?

30-19 The Outright Big Ten Football Champion in 2006 was the first since what year?

30-20 Name the five schools where Earle Bruce was a head football coach.

ANSWERS GROUP 30

30-1 Coaches Wes Fesler and Ernie Godfrey, Heisman Trophy winners Horvath, Janowicz, and Cassady

30-2 Warren Amling (1944-46)

30-3 At Penn State 63-14, 1994

30-4 Tippy Dye 1934-35-36

30-5 Bill Willis

30-6 Les Horvath 1944

30-7 1942 #1 National Champs

30-8 35 points

30-9 A major sports index ranking/polling organization since 1929

30-10 True

30-11 QB Troy Smith #10

30-12 Thurlow "Tad" Weed, place kicker on the 1954 National Championship Team

30-13 TRUE! Then Ohio State drove 99 yards to win the 1954 Big Ten Championship

30-14 342 yards vs. Norte Dame 2006 Fiesta Bowl

30-15 Texas (24-7), Michigan (42-39) and Florida (14-41)

30-16 False: He was the first!

30-17 Ted Ginn Jr.

30-18 All five were assistant coaches at Ohio State

30-19 1984

30-20 Tampa, Iowa State, Ohio State, Northern Iowa, and Colorado State

QUESTIONS **GROUP 31**

31-1 Name the three Buckeyes who have been second in the Heisman Trophy voting.

31-2 What was Troy Smith's winning percentage for the Heisman Trophy?

31-3 Ohio Stadium was built in 1922. What was the first year Wisconsin won in the "Shoe?"

31-4 Which MLB was on the U.S. Olympic boxing team and missed the 1998 season?

31-5 How many 200-yard games did Heisman Trophy winner Eddie George have in 1995?

31-6 Who was the first Buckeye to start in three Rose Bowl games?

31-7 What were "Groomer Boomers?"

31-8 Rex Kern, Art Schlichter, and Troy Smith, all QBs, wear what number?

31-9 **T or F** The Buckeyes lead the nation in attendance for 14 consecutive years from 1958 to 1971.

31-10 Which fullback was a bodyguard for "Ole Blue Eyes" Frank Sinatra?

31-11 In 2006, which team had greater attendance, Ohio State or Michigan?

31-12 **T or F** Ohio State was the first Big Ten school to win outright football and men's and women's basketball titles.

31-13 How many years has it been since the first pick in the NFL draft was an Ohio State linebacker?

31-14 Who was the first and only Buckeye QB to throw 4 TD passes in "The Game," with Michigan?

31-15 How many times (up to 2006) has Ohio State been ranked #1 in the pre-season?

31-16 What is Lloyd Carr's record for the last four years in his last two games from 2003-2006?

31-17 Who is the Ohio State Athletic Director that followed Andy Geiger?

31-18 **T or F** In 1946, Michigan leading 55-0, they kicked a field goal late in the game.

31-19 What was U of M Coach Bo Schembechler's Rose Bowl record after playing against Woody?

31-20 Which Ohio State football trainer is in the OSU Football Hall of Fame?

ANSWERS GROUP 31

31-1 Bob Ferguson (1961) to Ernie Davis; John Hicks (1973) to John Cappelletti and Keith Byers (1984) to Doug Flutie

31-2 86.7%

31-3 1982

31-4 MLB Derek Isaman

31-5 3-plus one for 314 yards against Illinois

31-6 John Hicks

31-7 Big punts by All-American Andy Groom

31-8 #10

31-9 True

31-10 Hubert Bobo

31-11 Michigan 1st (770,183), Penn State 2nd (752,972), and Ohio State 3rd (735,674)

31-12 True

31-13 26 years, 1980 Tom Cousineau; 2006 A J Hawk

31-14 QB Troy Smith #10, 2006

31-15 7 times

31-16 0-2 times 4 years equals 0-8; 4 losses to Ohio State and 4 losses in Bowl Games

31-17 Gene Smith from Arizona State

31-18 True: Woody went for 2 in 1968, winning 50-14

31-19 0-5

31-20 Ernie Biggs (1945-72) inducted in 1980

QUESTIONS GROUP 32

32-1 How many times was Troy Smith sacked by Florida's tackles in the BCS Championship game?

32-2 Which two Ohio State QBs have totaled over 400 yards in a game?

32-3 After beating Michigan 42-39 in 2006, how many games was Ohio State's win streak?

32-4 What was Earle Bruce's bowl game record?

32-5 How many Buckeyes were drafted by the NFL after the 2004 season?

32-6 What was Buckeye QB Craig Krenzel's major at Ohio State?

32-7 What is head coach Jim Tressel's full name?

32-8 Besides playing fullback, Hubert Bobo played what other position?

32-9 The latest "Michigan football team picture" shows nine Wolverines chasing who?

32-10 *Sporting News* magazine named which Buckeye "College Football Player of the Year" in 2006?

32-11 What years did Heisman Trophy winner "Hopalong" Cassady play baseball at Ohio State?

32-12 Which of the "Super Sophs" was the NFL's Rookie of the Year in 1971?

32-13 What three Ohio State assistant coaches are in the College Football Hall of Fame?

32-14 Who said, "This is not a game, this is war."

32-15 Who was the first Buckeye drafted in the NFL in 2007?

32-16 The saying, "Warfield was the Lighting, Ferguson is the Thunder" referred to what?

32-17 After "Spring Ball" 2007, who was the leading candidate to replace Heisman Trophy winner QB Troy Smith?

32-18 **T or F** After the 2007 NFL draft, Ohio State was number one in Number 1 picks for all-time.

32-19 What year did Ohio State change the color scheme for the "Horseshoe" field?

32-20 Who are the two young Buckeye boys on top of Pinnacle Peak, Scottsdale, AZ doing the famous O-H-I-O cheer with their girlfriends in the now famous picture?

ANSWERS GROUP 32

32-1   5 times Derrick Harvey (3), Jarvis Moss (2)
Only 13 times all season

32-2   Art Schlicter (412 yards, Florida State 1981),
Troy Smith (408 yards, Notre Dame 2006)

32-3   19

32-4   12-5

32-5   14

32-6   Molecular Genetics

32-7   James Patrick Tressel

32-8   Punter

32-9   Antonio Pittman on his 56-yard touchdown run in 2006

32-10 QB Troy Smith #10, 2006

32-11 1954-55-56

32-12 FB John Brockington (Green Bay Packers)

32-13 Doyt Perry, Ernie Godfrey and Sid Gillman

32-14 Woody Hayes, about the Michigan rivalry

32-15 Ted Ginn Jr. (Miami Dolphins)

32-16 The 1961 backfield of Bob Ferguson, Paul Warfield, and
Matt Snell

32-17 QB Todd Boeckman

32-18 True! When Anthony Gonzalez was selected the number was 66.

32-19 2007 Scarlet end zones and Block "O" on the fifty yard line

32-20 Jimmy and John McGuire, Columbus, Ohio, Upper Arlington
High School Grads

QUESTIONS GROUP 33

33-1   What was Troy Smith's pass/complication stat in the BCS Championship Game?

33-2   The Buckeyes have set the modern-day NFL draft record at how many players?

33-3   What was QB Troy Smith's career record as a Buckeye starter?

33-4   Who was named the 2006 Big Ten's Offensive Player of the Year?

33-5   What was the official attendance of the 2007 "Spring Ball" game April 21, 2007?

33-6   Which website runs a meter showing "Days since Michigan's Last Victory over Ohio State?"

33-7   Woody would be shocked! Starting in 2007, what can't coaches do between themselves and recruits per NCAA rules?

33-8   Who was the basketball great in 1962 that was the last man cut by the Cleveland Browns?

33-9   What four colors are on a Buckeye helmet?

33-10   **T or F**   The sousaphone player in TBDBITL can only dot the "i" once in their career.

33-11   Fred Cornell composed *Carmen Ohio* in 1902 after what occurrence?

33-12   Who is the only Heisman Trophy winner who did not play the previous season?

33-13   LB James Laurinaitis' dad, Joe, was a professional wrestler. His name was "Animal" and he was a member of which tag team?

33-14   Who is the only player to have his number retired that has not won the Heisman Trophy at Ohio State?

33-15   What was Mike Nugent's career field goal kicking percentage?

33-16   Who stated he was going "bald" because of too many 3rd and 1's?

33-17   What was Two-Time All-American, two-way lineman Jim Parker's number?

33-18   What was called "one of the greatest feats in American sports?"

33-19   Who was the Michigan player in 1969 that scored on a 60-yard punt return, and had three interceptions in Michigan's 24-12 victory over Ohio State?

33-20   Who lead Ohio State with interceptions (5 of 21) in 2006?

ANSWERS GROUP 33

33-1   4 for 14, for 35 yards and 1 interception

33-2   14 players, 2004

33-3   25-3

33-4   QB Troy Smith #10

33-5   75,301 WOW!

33-6   www.buckeyextra.com

33-7   Text messages…No electronically transmitted correspondence

33-8   John "Hondo" Havlicek, a basketball question, but one every Ohio State fan should know!

33-9   Silver helmet with red, white, and black center strips. Decorated with Buckeye leaves!

33-10   True! Only once!

33-11   86-0 loss to Michigan

33-12   Les Horvath, 1944

33-13   Road Warriors

33-14   Chic Harley

33-15   .857%

33-16   FB Jim Otis

33-17   62

33-18   Vic Janowicz, 21-yard field goal in the "Snow Bowl" game 1950

33-19   Barry Pierson

33-20   LB James Laurinaitis

QUESTIONS GROUP 34

34-1 What was *SI's* pre-season prediction for the Buckeyes in 2007, after the BCS loss to Florida?

34-2 What four players were taken in the first round of the NFL draft in 1971?

34-3 QB Troy Smith won which national quarterback award in 2006?

34-4 Who are the only father and son combinations to ever win National Football Championships?

34-5 Name the four players who ran on the 1993, 400-relay team to help Ohio State win a Big Ten title.

34-6 Starting in 2007, "The Kick-off" will be from what yard line?

34-7 Carrying one of these in your pocket brings good luck. What is it?

34-8 Who is the only running back to lead the Buckeyes in rushing four times?

34-9 What safety was named the National Defensive Player of the Year during his senior season?

34-10 How many times did Coach Cooper win in Ann Arbor?

34-11 What animal does the "Illibuck" represent?

34-12 How many Buckeyes were drafted in 2007?

34-13 Which Buckeye has won three Super Bowl rings?

34-14 What was the headline on the *Columbus Dispatch* newspaper following the 2006 win over Michigan?

34-15 Coach Tressel believes in 'what play' as the biggest play in football?

34-16 Which WR caught nine passes for 253 yards in a 54-14 win over Pittsburgh in 1995?

34-17 Who lived in the White House the last time (before 2006) the Buckeyes beat a top-five ranked Michigan team?

34-18 **T or F** Coming into the 2006 Ohio State-Michigan game, Michigan was No. 1 in third-down defense, OSU No. 1 in interceptions, with 21.

34-19 In Super Bowl III, which former Buckeye ran for 121 yards and 40 yards receiving to help the Jets upset the Colts?

34-20 In 2006, who was the only undefeated Division 1-A team?

ANSWERS GROUP 34

34-1   #4, Wisconsin #6 and Michigan #7

34-2   Tim Anderson, John Brockington, Leo Hayden, and Jack Tatum

34-3   The Davey O'Brien Foundation

34-4   Head Coaches Lee and Jim Tressel

34-5   Butler By'not'e, Aaron Payne, Chris Sanders, and Robert Smith

34-6   30-yard line. Hopefully to cut back on touch-backs and get more returns

34-7   A Buckeye

34-8   Archie Griffin, 1972-1975

34-9   Jack Tatum 1970

34-10 Zero—never

34-11 A turtle

34-12 8

34-13 Mike Vrabel, with the New England Patriots

34-14 In bold lettering: ONE TO GO!

34-15 The PUNT!

34-16 Terry Glenn

34-17 President Gerald Ford, a Michigan center and MVP

34-18 True

34-19 Matt Snell

34-20 Boise State (13-0)

QUESTIONS GROUP 35

35-1 **T or F** The greatest track star of all-time, Jesse Owens, played WR for the 1935 Buckeyes.

35-2 True Buckeye fans consider the most irritating college football announcer to be Lee Corso or Brent Musburger?

35-3 What is the largest student organization at The Ohio State University?

35-4 Who was the first Ohio State head coach to receive a Top 10 National ranking?

35-5 Who was the Big Ten Defensive Player of the Year in 1996?

35-6 What is Ohio State's record against SEC teams in Bowl Games?

35-7 What was the per team pay-out for the BCS National Championship Game, Ohio State vs. Florida?

35-8 Which RB had the greater average per carry in 2006, Pittman or Wells?

35-9 What makes Buckeye nuts poisonous to humans, horses, and cattle?

35-10 What high school did QB Troy Smith and WR Ted Ginn Jr. attend?

35-11 In the 2006 Texas game #1 vs. #2, who caused a fumble and had an interception?

35-12 Who holds the single season record for pass receptions and yards?

35-13 Of the 12 leading stats for passing yards per season, which three QBs did it twice?

35-14 What is RB Chris Wells' nickname?

35-15 Who won the 2006 Bill Willis Award as the Bucks Outstanding Defensive Player of the Year?

35-16 Who did Florida beat in the SEC Championship game to get to Glendale, AZ to play in the BCS National Championship game?

35-17 Where and when did Florida head coach Urban Meyer start his coaching career?

35-18 43 of his 49 catches resulted in what for Anthony Gonzalez in 2006?

35-19 When was the last time the Buckeyes scored 80 points plus?

35-20 **T or F** OSU played in a three time over-time, a two time over-time and a one time over-time game.

ANSWERS GROUP 35

35-1 False: There were no wide receivers in 1935 and Jesse Owens did not play football.

35-2 Brent Musburger

35-3 Block "O", started in 1938

35-4 Francis Schmidt

35-5 CB Shawn Springs

35-6 0-8

35-7 $17 million

35-8 Chris Wells, 5.5 to 5.1 yards per carry

35-9 Tannic acid

35-10 Glenville High School, Cleveland, Ohio

35-11 LB James Laurinaitis

35-12 David Boston, 85 receptions, 1,435 yards, 1998

35-13 Jim Karsatos 85-86, Bobby Hoying 94-95, Troy Smith 05-06

35-14 "Beanie"

35-15 Quinn Pitcock, All-American

35-16 Arkansas 38-28

35-17 Ohio State, Graduate Assistant under Earle Bruce, 1986

35-18 First downs

35-19 83 points against Iowa, 1950

35-20 True: Won 44-38 NCS, Won 31-24 Miami, Loss 33-27 NW

QUESTIONS GROUP 36

36-1 What year did Brutus Buckeye show up in the "Horseshoe?"

36-2 Which RB came off the bench and scored three touchdowns against Indiana in his first game?

36-3 **T or F** Between 1934 and 2002 (68 years), Ohio State did not play an in-state road trip game.

36-4 Which QB threw for more yards in their senior season, Troy Smith (2006) or Joe Germaine (1998)?

36-5 What was the last game played at Ohio Field in 1921?

36-6 Which QB holds the Buckeye record for rushing touchdowns in a season?

36-7 After the 2006 season, what is the number of straight wins in Buckeye Home Openers?

36-8 Who was the last player to intercept a pass in four consecutive ball games?

36-9 What is the website for the Big Ten Conference?

36-10 How many Big Ten teams went to Bowl Games in the 2006 season?

36-11 What is the name of the new field installed in the "Horseshoe" in 2007?

36-12 How many different ways did Ted Ginn Jr. score a touchdown at Ohio State?

36-13 From what Columbus high school did Ohio State and Minnesota Viking great Jim Marshall graduate?

36-14 In 2007, who was the latest Buckeye to be inducted into the College Football Hall of Fame?

36-15 How many defensive starters did Coach Tressel have to replace in 2006?

36-16 In 2006 Michigan lead the nation in rushing defense at 29.9 yards; how many yards did the Buckeyes rush against them in their 42-39 victory?

36-17 Who was Woody's first All-American quarterback?

36-18 Who lead the 2006 defense with 100 tackles and five interceptions?

36-19 Who was the favorite to take the Youngstown head coaching job when Jim Tressel was chosen in 1986?

36-20 What was Texas' win streak when Ohio State stopped them in 2006?

ANSWERS **GROUP 36**

36-1   1965

36-2   Howard "Hopalong" Cassady, Heisman Trophy winner, 1955

36-3   True

36-4   Joe Germaine, 3,240 yards vs. Troy Smith 2,507 yards

36-5   Illinois vs. Ohio State. A loss for the Buckeyes.

36-6   Les Horvath 14, 1944, also a running back beside the QB

36-7   28 straight

36-8   LB James Laurinaitis, 2006 Texas, Cincinnati, Penn State, and Iowa

36-9   www.bigten.org

36-10 Seven teams

36-11 FieldTurf

36-12 5 ways: rushing, receiving, throwing, punt and kick-off returns

36-13 Columbus East High School, 1956

36-14 QB Rex Kern

36-15 Nine players, including all of the back seven

36-16 187 yards and threw for four touchdowns

36-17 Rex Kern

36-18 LB James Laurinaitis

36-19 Gerry Faust

36-20 21 games

QUESTIONS GROUP 37

37-1 When does the planting of a buckeye tree in the Buckeye Grove to honor All-Americans occur?

37-2 Vic Janowicz punted how many times and for how many yards in the 1950 "Snow Bowl" game?

37-3 After which game did Coach Hayes state "We're becoming quite a passing team."?

37-4 Have any Ohio State Heisman Trophy winners won a Super Bowl?

37-5 From 1981-1987, which Big Ten team beat the Buckeyes five times?

37-6 How many times did Woody and "Bear" Bryant coach against each other?

37-7 What season did OSU have four straight 40-point games?

37-8 In 2006, how many times did QB Troy Smith win Big Ten Offensive Payer of the Week?

37-9 For most true Buckeye fans, what are the Top 3 most disliked teams?

37-10 Who lead the nation in punt-return average as a freshman (25.6 yards)?

37-11 In which game did James Lauriniatis have his first career interception?

37-12 When Ohio State beat #13 Iowa in 2006, their nation-leading win streak stood at what number?

37-13 In 2006, OSU had their first shutout since 2003. Who was that team?

37-14 Who was the first Ohio State head coach to have two 12-win seasons?

37-15 What was the score of the 2005 Texas game in Columbus?

37-16 When Ohio State first played Michigan in 1897, how many points for a TD, and how many points for the conversion?

37-17 What was Michigan head coach Fielding Yost's nickname?

37-18 What OSU great was the AFL Rookie of the Year in 1964 with the New York Jets?

37-19 What year was the first time the Buckeyes and the Wolverines entered into their game with undefeated teams?

37-20 What year did the Buckeyes tear down the "M CLUB SUPPORTS YOU" banner in Ann Arbor?

ANSWERS GROUP 37

37-1   Just prior to the Spring Ball game.

37-2   Punted 21 times for 685 yards, a 33-yard average

37-3   1968 over SMU 35-14, SMU was 37/69, 417 yards;
       Ohio State was 8/14, 227 yards

37-4   Not yet, but it will happen some day.

37-5   Wisconsin

37-6   Once, 1977 Sugar Bowl, Alabama won 35-6

37-7   2005, Indiana (41 points), Minnesota (45 points),
       Illinois (40 points), Northwestern (48 points)

37-8   Five times

37-9   Michigan (M), Notre Dame (ND) and Southern California (USC)

37-10 Ted Ginn Jr.

37-11 Texas 2006, plus two forced fumbles and 13 tackles

37-12 12th

37-13 Minnesota 44-0

37-14 Jim Tressel, 2002, 2006

37-15 25-22

37-16 4 points for a TD; 2 points for a conversion.
       Final Score: 34-0 Michigan

37-17 "Hurry Up"

37-18 FB Matt Snell

37-19 1970 Ohio State Victory 20-9

37-20 1973, the 10-10 Tie Game

QUESTIONS **GROUP 38**

38-1 Between 1937 and 1957 how many times did Michigan lose to OSU in Ann Arbor?

38-2 With which team does Ohio State have their longest running continuous series?

38-3 Which Ohio State defensive coordinator in the modern era played tight end for Ohio State?

38-4 Ohio State allowed how many points in the first half against Florida, the most since the 1977 Sugar Bowl loss against Alabama 30 years before?

38-5 **T or F** In three wins against Michigan QB Troy Smith had over 1,000 yards, seven TD passes and one rushing TD?

38-6 What was the score when #1 Ohio State beat #2 Texas in 2006?

38-7 Who lead the country in kick returns in 2005 as a sophomore?

38-8 **T or F** Ohio State held opponents to less than 100 yards on punt returns in 2006?

38-9 Who was the first sophomore in the history of football to win the Bronko Nagurski trophy?

38-10 How many times was Jim Tressel National Runner-up at Youngstown State?

38-11 **T or F** The Ohio State vs. Texas game 9-9-06 was the largest crowd in Texas football history?

38-12 What game was Anthony Gonzalez's career high for catches?

38-13 What is the Ohio State record crowd in the "Horseshoe"?

38-14 Who said "I think he is the best player in college football"?

38-15 The 81 combined points in the 2006 Michigan game was the most since which game?

38-16 Who is the Buckeye leader for punt return yards in a single season?

38-17 What was Ohio States final AP and USA Today ranking in 2005?

38-18 Who was the quickest head coach to get to 50 wins for the Ohio State Buckeyes?

38-19 What was the final score in the 1978 Gator Bowl against the Clemson Tigers?

38-20 Who said "Without winners, there wouldn't even be civilization"?

ANSWERS GROUP 38

38-1   Once in 1957, Buckeyes won 31-14

38-2   Illinois, since 1914

38-3   Fred Pagac

38-4   34 points, final score 41-14

38-5   True: 1,051 total yards

38-6   Ohio State 24, Texas 7

38-7   Ted Ginn Jr.

38-8   TRUE 91 yards

38-9   LB James Laurinaitis 2006

38-10   Twice 1992 and 1999, four times National Champion 1991, 1993, 1994, and 1997

38-11   TRUE 89,422 in attendance. Ohio State 24, Texas 7

38-12   Texas with eight receptions for 142 yards and one touchdown

38-13   105,708 vs. Michigan 2006

38-14   Jim Tressel speaking of QB Troy Smith, 2006

38-15   1902 Michigan victory 86-0

38-16   Neal Colzie, 673 yards, 1979

38-17   #4 10-2, Penn State #3 11-1, Michigan not ranked

38-18   Jim Tressel, only four others have 50+ wins: Wilce, Hayes, Bruce, and Cooper

38-19   17-15; a Buckeye loss

38-20   Head Coach Woody Hayes

QUESTIONS **GROUP 39**

39-1 What year did the Ohio State Faculty Council vote 28 to 25 to NOT attend the Rose Bowl?

39-2 Which Northern Illinois RB ran for 171 yards against the Buckeyes in their 2006 opener?

39-3 How long was Ted Ginn Jr.'s opening kick-off return in the BCS game against Florida?

39-4 Who kicked the winning field goal in the 1958 Rose Bowl to beat Oregon 10-7?

39-5 Which Buckeye had 260 all-purpose yards against Notre Dame in the 2005 Fiesta Bowl?

39-6 All-American Quinn Pitcock led the 2006 Buckeyes in what category?

39-7 **T or F** The turnover margin was +11 in 2005, and –9 in 2006.

39-8 What number does LB James Lauriniatis wear?

39-9 What color is the visitor's locker room, including toilets and urinals at Iowa?

39-10 After the 1984 outright Big Ten title, how long did it take to win another outright title?

39-11 **T or F** When Michigan Stadium opened in 1927, was it the largest college stadium at that time?

39-12 In Woody's first 18 years, how many times did Michigan win the Big Ten title?

39-13 Because of the No-Repeat rule, who went to the Rose Bowl in 1955 after Ohio State beat Michigan for the Big Ten Championship?

39-14 What year was the first game with Michigan where the winner would be the outright Big Ten Champion?

39-15 In 2000, which players were selected the Co-Captains for the All-Century Team?

39-16 How many times did Archie Griffin score in his four games with Michigan?

39-17 **T or F** In the OSU losses to Texas and Penn State in 2005, OSU had less than 300 yards offense per game.

39-18 Which team was voted "College Football Team of the Decade?"

39-19 What was Michigan's record against OSU through 1927 when they opened Michigan Stadium?

39-20 What was the four-year win-loss record for the senior class of 2006?

ANSWERS GROUP 39

39-1 1961

39-2 Garrett Wolfe, WOW!

39-3 93 yards

39-4 Don Sutherin

39-5 Ted Ginn Jr., 34-10 victory for the Buckeyes

39-6 QB sacks with eight

39-7 False: just the opposite +11 in 2006, −9 in 2005

39-8 33

39-9 Pink!

39-10 2006, 22 years

39-11 True

39-12 One time in 1964

39-13 Michigan State Spartans

39-14 1944, Ohio State 19 Michigan 14. Heisman Trophy winner Les Horvath scoring the winning touchdown.

39-15 Chris Spielman and Jack Tatum, Defense; Archie Griffin and Rex Kern, Offense

39-16 One game, 1972; Ohio State 14, Michigan 11

39-17 True: Texas 255 yards; Penn State 230 yards

39-18 1968 National Champions

39-19 19-3-2

39-20 40-8, four Bowl Games, three BCS Games and two Big Ten Titles

QUESTIONS GROUP 40

40-1   Which Big Ten team has the largest print and internet media following?

40-2   Which linebacker holds the record for the most tackles for a loss in a single season?

40-3   Who was the first head coach to Beat Michigan in 1919?

40-4   Between 1890 (OSU's first season) and 1912, how many head coaches did Ohio State have?

40-5   Which head coach with at least three seasons coaching has the highest winning percentage?

40-6   Through 2006, what is the combined win/loss record vs. Michigan for Coach Bruce, Cooper and Tressel?

40-7   Which head coach left and came back two years later?

40-8   How many players who played for Woody were drafted in the first round of the NFL draft?

40-9   How many seasons has Ohio State had two or more first round NFL draft picks?

40-10 Which season resulted in the highest number of players drafted?

40-11 What was Ohio State's first 10-win season and how many have they had since (including 2006)?

40-12 Has Ohio State ever had a no-win season?

40-13 What are the most ties Ohio State has had in a season?

40-14 For 1-A Division teams, which team has the highest winning percentage in the last 77 years?

40-15 **T or F**   Have Ohio State football and basketball teams ever been ranked #1 at the same time?

40-16 Who said upon his hiring as head coach, "I'm not coming here for security; I came here for the opportunity."?

40-17 **T or F**   During "The Ten Year War" 1969-1978, OSU always played before 103,000 plus fans in Ann Arbor.

40-18 In "The Ten Year War" was Ohio State ever not ranked?

40-19 What was the "team slogan" for the 2006 Buckeye team?

40-20 What three articles of clothing would Woody destroy in a fit of anger?

ANSWERS GROUP 40

40-1   The Ohio State Buckeyes

40-2   Andy Katzenmoyer

40-3   John Wilce

40-4   11, 5 of which only stayed 1 season

40-5   Jim Tressel thru 2006 .816%

40-6   12-15-1 vs. Woody's record of 16-11-1, both 28 years

40-7   Coach Jack Ryder, 1892-95 returned 1898

40-8   29

40-9   15 seasons

40-10   2004, 14 players

40-11   1954, 16 seasons

40-12   NO! But 2 seasons were 1 win seasons, 1890 & 1897

40-13   3, 1910, 1924, 1932

40-14   Ohio State #1 .74185%, Michigan is third behind Oklahoma .72649%

40-15   True: 2006/07 Both lost National Championship games

40-16   Woody Hayes, 1951

40-17   True: and played in front of 87,000+ in Columbus

40-18   Yes! 1971

40-19   "Just One Agenda"

40-20   Tear and throw his hat, throw his watch, and stomp on his glasses!

QUESTIONS **GROUP 41**

41-1   Who did Head Coach Jim Tressel beat for his 200th win?

41-2   How many head coaches did Ohio State have prior to Jim Tressel?

41-3   What yard-line change occurred with the rule change for kick-offs in 2007?

41-4   Americasbestonline.net list of the Greatest Football Players of 2007 included how many Buckeyes? Name them!

41-5   Who did the Associated Press name as the NFL Offensive Rookie of the Year in 1971?

41-6   Who was the seventh great Buckeye player to have his number retired in 2007?

41-7   **T or F**   Ohio State has a 2-to-1 winning edge over Purdue at Lafayette, Indiana.

41-8   What year was the first All-American Team for all-college football named?

41-9   Name the top three non-football sports stars at The Ohio State University.

41-10   Who set the record of playing in 141 consecutive games at the cornerback position in the NFL?

41-11   What is another name for the goal posts?

41-12   What year did the rule change where a quarterback could become a receiver?

41-13   Who won the 2007 Butkus Award?

41-14   What famous Ohio murder trial was going on during the 1954 championship season?

41-15   Which Ohio State player was its first three-time winner and a charter member inducted into the College Football Hall of Fame?

41-16   What are the two types of turnovers in college football?

41-17   Who was the first OSU lineman and defensive player to have his number retired?

41-18   Who is known as the "Father of American Football?"

41-19   Who is the highest paid center in NFL history?

41-20   Which player won a National Championship in 1957 at Ohio State and an NFL Championship at Cleveland in 1964?

ANSWERS GROUP 41

41-1   The University of Washington Huskies, 9-15-2007, 33-14

41-2   21 head coaches, Jim Tressel was #22 starting in 2001

41-3   Moved back from the 35-yard line to the 30-yard line

41-4   Seven: Griffin, Parker, Pace, Spielman, Tatum, Gradishar and Hicks

41-5   John Brockington, Green Bay Packers

41-6   "The Ultimate Buckeye," #99, Bill Willis

41-7   True: 12-6 as of 2007

41-8   1889

41-9   Jesse Owens (track), Jack Nicklaus (golf), John Havlicek (basketball)

41-10 Dick LeBeau

41-11 Uprights

41-12 1967

41-13 LB James Laurinaitis

41-14 Dr. Sam Sheppard in Cleveland, Ohio

41-15 Charles Wesley "Chic" Harley

41-16 Fumble or Pass Interception

41-17 Bill Willis, #99, learned about it October 5, 2007, his 86th birthday, ceremony on November 3, 2007

41-18 Walter Camp, he also choose the first All-American Team

41-19 LeCharles Bentley

41-20 Tackle, Dick Schafrath

QUESTIONS GROUP 42

42-1   The Woody Hayes Trophy for the College Football Coach of the Year is presented by which organization?

42-2   What was Jim Tressel's record in the 1990s at Youngstown State?

42-3   What two Big Ten schools do not have a mascot?

42-4   Which Heisman Memorial Trophy winner won the first Chic Harley Award for the College Football Player of the Year?

42-5   Which "Razzle-Dazzle" head coach was nicknamed "Close the Gates of Mercy?"

42-6   **T or F** Tressels' teams have held their opponents to less than 10 yards rushing.

42-7   What two brothers from Akron played against each other in "The Game" of 1957?

42-8   If a defensive player returns a blocked kick, or intercepted pass on a conversion attempt to the other end zone, what is it worth?

42-9   What was Woody's record in the first year of his 28 years at The Ohio State University?

42-10 What was the most important play in the 2002 National Championship season?

42-11 "Hop" Cassady held what three career records for decades before they were surpassed?

42-12 What are the two kinds of "clocks" used in a college football game?

42-13 Which Buckeye set the record for the most yards on punt returns as a rookie in the NFL?

42-14 Which OSU QB held the Ohio high hchool record for career passing yards at 10,500?

42-15 Which Buckeye made the AFL's All-Time Team and played in two Super Bowls as an offensive tackle?

42-16 Who established the Anne and Woody Hayes Endowment for the Prevention of Child Abuse at the Columbus Children's Hospital?

42-17 Taking the three year records of 2005-06-07, which team had the best winning percentage in the country?

42-18 How old was walk-on place kicker Ryan Pretorius from Durban, South Africa in the 2008 BCS Championship Game against LSU?

42-19 How many of the No. 2 ranked teams lost during the regular season in 2007?

42-20 Which Ohio State assistant coach won the 12th Broyles Award for nation's top assistant?

ANSWERS GROUP 42

42-1 Touchdown Club of Columbus, founded in 1956 by Sam B. Nicola

42-2 103-27-2

42-3 Indiana (Hoosiers), Michigan (Wolverines) use nicknames; NO MASCOTS!

42-4 HB Howard "Hopalong" Cassady, #40, 1955

42-5 Francis Schmidt

42-6 True: several games and counting!

42-7 Tom Baldacci (Ohio State) and Lou Baldacci (Michigan). Ohio State won 17-0 and the National Championship

42-8 2 points, in 1992 it also included a fumble return from outside the end zone

42-9 4-3-2 1951, Woody was 17-0 at Denison 1947-1948

42-10 *Author's Opinion:* Chris Gamble's interception and 40-yard return for a touchdown against Penn State, winning 13-7. Question open for discussion!

42-11 Career rushing yards (2,466); scoring points (222); all-purpose yards (4,403)

42-12 Game clock (60 minutes); play clock (40 seconds to run a play)

42-13 Neal Colzie, 1975 Oakland Raiders, 655 yards

42-14 Justin Swick

42-15 Jim Tyrer, Kansas City Chiefs

42-16 QB Rex Kern, #10, 1968-1970

42-17 Ohio State .892% (33-4), followed by West Virginia .888% (32-4) and four teams at .865% (32-5) Texas, Boise State, LSU and USC

42-18 28 years old—a junior at that!

42-19 Seven: USC, California, South Florida, Boston College, Oregon, Kansas and West Virginia

42-20 Jim Heacock, Ohio State Defensive Coordinator

QUESTIONS GROUP 43

43-1 What fraternity at Baldwin-Wallace was Head Coach Jim Tressel a member?

43-2 Woody Hayes stated, "The best linebacker I ever coached." Who was he speaking about?

43-3 Who said, "Football is a game that is every bit as mental as it is physical?"

43-4 What occupation does Brian Robiskie's father perform?

43-5 Which team holds the record for the most weeks being ranked No. 1 in the BCS polls?

43-6 Who broke "Chic" Harley's individual scoring record?

43-7 Who was the first African-American to play for Head Coach Francis Schmidt?

43-8 In college football, what color are the two flags that are used, and what are they used for?

43-9 Which Ohio State coach is the only one undefeated at Massillon High School?

43-10 Which Buckeye is one of twelve players to play all ten years of the AFL's existence?

43-11 Which Ohio State head coach played with Jim Thorpe and the Canton Bull Dogs, winning the Pro Football Championship in 1917?

43-12 How many times was coach Jim Tressel Division 1-AA National Coach of the Year?

43-13 Name the four Ohio born coaches in the Top 8 BCS teams at the end of 2006?

43-14 **T or F** Since 1949, Ohio State has never been ranked lower than fourth nationally in average home attendance.

43-15 Who was Ohio State's Academic All-American of the Year?

43-16 What two former Ohio State All-American linebackers wore the same number in the NFL during the 2007-2008 seasons?

43-17 Which LSU player was suspended for 12 games, yet got a clearance and blocked a field goal in the BCS National Championship Game of 2008?

43-18 Who holds the record for the longest field goal in Rose Bowl history?

43-19 What game was called the "Quagmire Bowl?"

43-20 What is the "open door policy" at Ohio State?

ANSWERS GROUP 43

43-1 Alpha Tau Omega (ATO)

43-2 LB Randy Gradishar, 1971-1973

43-3 Head Coach Woody Hayes, 1957

43-4 An NFL Assistant Coach

43-5 The Ohio State University Buckeyes

43-6 HB Howard "Hopalong" Cassady, #40 in 1955

43-7 Bill Willis, 1940

43-8 Yellow (Officials for Penalties); Red (Coach's Challenge)

43-9 Earle Bruce, undefeated 1964-1965

43-10 Ernie Wright

43-11 Sam Willaman, Head Coach 1929-1933

43-12 Four times at Youngstown State

43-13 Jim Tressel (Ohio State), Berea; Les Miles (LSU), Elyria; Gary Pinkel (Missouri), Akron; Bob Stoops (Oklahoma), Youngstown

43-14 True: The "Horseshoe" has a current capacity of 102,329

43-15 QB Craig Krenzel, 2003

43-16 #50: A.J. Hawk, Green Bay Packers; Mike Vrabel, New England Patriots

43-17 Jean Francois, #90

43-18 Rick Spangler, 52 yards, 1985 Rose Bowl vs. USC, losing 20-17

43-19 The 1958 Rose Bowl won by the National Champion Ohio State Buckeyes over USC 20-7 in a downpour.

43-20 W-I-D-E, gaping holes in the line for running backs to run through!

QUESTIONS **GROUP 44**

44-1 Which coach got his 200th win the same day Jim Tressel won his 200th game?

44-2 What year was the "Pay-Back" game in the Michigan rivalry?

44-3 Which Big Ten school plays in a dome stadium?

44-4 What year did Ohio State begin to play in the Western Conference (later the Big Ten)?

44-5 Which All-American tackle (1973) won the Lombardi Award and Outland Trophy?

44-6 Who set the Ohio State record for the longest punt return against Kent State in 2007?

44-7 Who was the last team to beat Ohio State in the "Horseshoe" when Ohio State was ranked No. 1?

44-8 Which running back (through 2007) has carried the ball the most times on average per game?

44-9 Who was the Big Ten's MVP and Silver Football Trophy winner as a sophomore in 1945?

44-10 Who is considered the greatest fullback in Ohio State football history?

44-11 What former Buckeye QB (1934-35-36) became the head basketball coach at Ohio State 1947-1950?

44-12 What four things occur to end a play?

44-13 Who was the first African-American QB at Ohio State, and was also the Rose Bowl MVP in 1974?

44-14 Who was the Cincinnati Bengals first No. 1 overall draft pick in their history?

44-15 Through 2007, how many Buckeyes have won the Big Ten Silver Football for MVP?

44-16 Since its inception in 1998, how many Big Ten teams have played for the National Championship in the BCS?

44-17 What was the final score in the 2008 BCS National Championship Game vs. LSU?

44-18 What was the first year Ohio State averaged over 100,000 fans per game in the "Shoe?"

44-19 What year did Ohio State first play football, and what was their record?

44-20 **T or F** It has been written that Michigan used "tramp" players in the 1890s to win several games for coach Fielding Yost.

Go Bucks!™ **BEAT MICHIGAN**®

ANSWERS GROUP 44

44-1   Head Coach Frank Beamer, Virginia Tech

44-2   1970, Ohio State 21-Michigan 7, for the previous year upset loss 24-12 in Ann Arbor

44-3   Minnesota Gophers in the Metrodome

44-4   1913, with John Wilce as Head Coach

44-5   Tackle John Hicks

44-6   Brian Hartline, a 48-3 victory

44-7   1998, Michigan State Spartans, 28-24

44-8   Keith Byars in 1984, 28 carries per game!

44-9   Ollie Cline, 936 yards rushing, 9 touchdowns

44-10 Bob Ferguson 1959-1961, two-time All-American, second in the Heisman Trophy and winner of the Maxwell Trophy

44-11 "Tippy" Dye, won a Big Ten Basketball Championship in 1950

44-12 Tackle, incomplete pass, out of bounds and scoring points

44-13 QB Cornelius Green

44-14 Dan Wilkinson, 1994

44-15 15: tied with Michigan at the moment

44-16 One team ONLY, The Ohio State University Buckeyes through 2008

44-17 38-24, LSU winning its third National Championship

44-18 2001, 103,532 Buckeye FANS!

44-19 1890, Ohio State beating Ohio Wesleyan 20-14, May 3, 1890, 0-3 for games played in November of that year

44-20 True: Ohio State has never been accused of using "tramp" players to win games

QUESTIONS GROUP 45

45-1   What was the 500th game in the Ohio Stadium "Horseshoe?"

45-2   Which stadiums in the Big Ten are named "Memorial?"

45-3   Between 1956 and 1966, how many three-game losing streaks did Woody Hayes coach?

45-4   **T or F**   The height of the crossbar on the goal post has always been 10 feet high.

45-5   Woody Hayes said, "When (who) got in front of our bench he turned on all the jets?"

45-6   Which of Woody's players epitomized the "Triple-Threat" football player?

45-7   Who was the QB of the "Super-Sophomores" and what was their three-year record?

45-8   Name the five "special" player positions.

45-9   Which U.S. President threatened to ban football because of growing violence and death?

45-10 Which QB led Ohio State to two great comebacks: 33-20 deficit against LSU, winning 36-33; 31-0 deficit against Minnesota winning 41-37?

45-11 Who was the leading tackler in the 2002 BCS National Championship Game against the University of Miami Hurricanes?

45-12 How many Big Ten Championship title teams did Rex Kern quarterback?

45-13 Ohio State led the Big Ten in 2006 with the All-Academic Team. How many years have they done this?

45-14 Of the top ten rushing performances at Ohio State, name the three running backs that have two each.

45-15 Which year will Ohio State start to play Michigan *after* Thanksgiving because of Big Ten Conference rescheduling?

45-16 In 2004, what bowl game did Coach Les Miles lose to Jim Tressel?

45-17 Which Ohio State head coach proved a non-eastern coach could be successful at the college football game?

45-18 Who said, "They'll have to wrench a playoff system out of my cold, dead hands?"

45-19 Who won Ohio State's first Conference Championship with a 7-0 record and repeated the next season 8-0-1?

45-20 What season did 20 top ten teams and 13 top five teams lose to unranked teams?

ANSWERS GROUP 45

45-1 Ohio State vs. Northwestern, September 22, 2007; Ohio State 58-NW 7

45-2 Indiana and Illinois

45-3 None

45-4 True: the uprights distance has changed a few times over history

45-5 "Hop" Cassady on his famous interception of 88 yards against Wisconsin, October 23, 1954

45-6 Vic Janowicz, 1950 Heisman Memorial Trophy winner

45-7 Rex Kern, 1968-1970, record 27-2, inductee into College Football Hall of Fame 2007

45-8 Place kicker, punter, holder, long snapper and kick returner

45-9 President Theodore Roosevelt in 1906

45-10 Greg Frey

45-11 Matt Wilhelm, 11 tackles

45-12 Three consecutive teams, 1968-69-70

45-13 Five straight years led the Big Ten Conference, 2007 figures not out yet

45-14 Eddie George (314 and 219 yards), Archie Griffin (246 and 239), Chris Wells (222 and 221 yards)

45-15 2009

45-16 Alamo Bowl, Ohio State 33-Oklahoma State 7

45-17 Albert Herrnstein, 1906-1909, 28-10-1

45-18 Gordon Gee, President of the Ohio State University

45-19 John Wilce, 1916 and 1917

45-20 2007

QUESTIONS GROUP 46

46-1 Who did Head Coach Jim Tressel beat to win his first National Championship in 1991?

46-2 **T or F** John Cooper's loss in the 2000 Outback Bowl was to a ranked team.

46-3 Who was the Honorary Captain at the 2007 Ohio State vs. Washington game in Seattle?

46-4 What year and which head coach won Ohio State's first invitation to the Rose Bowl?

46-5 What is the longest punt return against Ohio State in the Modern Era?

46-6 In what year was the forward pass legalized to help cut down on injuries?

46-7 What are the five ways to score points in a college football game?

46-8 Head Coach Carroll Widdoes was an assistant to which fabled coach at Massillon, Ohio high school?

46-9 What is the correct nomenclature for "pay dirt?"

46-10 Who won his third National League (baseball) MVP Award the same year "Hop" Cassady won his Heisman Memorial Trophy?

46-11 In 1969, how many points did Ohio State average per game through its first eight games?

46-12 Which former Ohio State QB and Indiana head football coach highlight the ESPN "College Football Game Day" football show?

46-13 **T or F** The original Ohio State University Marching Band was an "all-brass band."

46-14 Which Buckeye holds the record for the shortest punt return for a TD in NFL history?

46-15 Who was the only player to win Ohio's Mr. Football Award twice?

46-16 In Coach Tressel's first victory against No. 11 Michigan in 2001, who ran for 129 yards and three touchdowns?

46-17 **T or F** Ohio State won the first MacArthur Trophy representing the National Championship.

46-18 Which was the first school to win the BCS National Championship twice?

46-19 How many College Hall of Fame players does Ohio State have through 2007?

46-20 Which All-American, College Hall of Fame, pro player was born in Ikaris, Greece?

ANSWERS GROUP 46

46-1 Marshall

46-2 False: Lou Holtz' South Carolina team was unranked

46-3 Former Athletic Director Andy Geiger

46-4 1920, John Wilce (7-1)

46-5 90 yards by Jim Saufner of TCU in 1957

46-6 1906, made famous by Knute Rockne in 1913;
Notre Dame-Army game upset 35-13

46-7 6 points (TD), 1 or 2 points (PAT), 3 points (Field Goal), 2 points
(Safety), 1 point (Forfeit)

46-8 Paul Brown

46-9 End Zone

46-10 Roy Campanella, Brooklyn Dodgers, 1955

46-11 46 points per game, before losing to Michigan 24-12

46-12 QB Kirk Herbstreit and Indiana Head Coach Lee Corso

46-13 False: it is now the largest all-brass band, but it started out
as a 12-piece fife and drum corps

46-14 Shaun Gayle, Chicago Bears, 1985, 5 yards

46-15 Robert Smith (1988 and 1989)

46-16 RB Jonathan Wells

46-17 False: Syracuse won it in 1959

46-18 LSU at Ohio State's expense in 2008. Ohio State is now
1-2 in BCS National Championship Games

46-19 21

46-20 Gust Zarnas, Born December 16, 1913, played from 1935-1937

QUESTIONS GROUP 47

47-1 At the time of the 500th game in Ohio Stadium, what was the team's record?

47-2 Tough defense, conservative ball-control offense, with a kicking game for field position is called what?

47-3 Whose bust will be on display at the new Sports Museum of America in New York City?

47-4 What was the record of the "Super-Sophomores" at The Ohio State University?

47-5 Which two Pro Football Hall of Fame players did Ohio State play against at Illinois in 1957?

47-6 Name the schools whose cheering sections are the "White Out," "Black Out" and "Gold Out."

47-7 Who broke Dave Francis' record for the most rushing yards against Michigan in 2007?

47-8 What two Bronko Nagurski Trophy Award winners played against each other in the BCS Championship Game in 2008?

47-9 QB Rex Kern beat which Heisman Trophy winner and lost to which one in the Rose Bowl games?

47-10 Which three-time consensus All-American football player was Ohio State's first All-American basketball player?

47-11 What award recognizes OSU football's MVP for the entire season—after the bowl games?

47-12 What three Ohio State kickers have kicked five field goals in a single game?

47-13 Which Buckeye RB scored three touchdowns and was the MVP in the U.S Army All-American Bowl in 2005?

47-14 What was the forerunner of the modern day middle linebacker?

47-15 Which OSU All-American, College Hall of Fame player became a Doctor of Veterinary Medicine?

47-16 How many undefeated seasons and one-loss seasons did Woody Hayes coach?

47-17 Which hotel did Woody Hayes take his Rose Bowl teams to in Los Angeles?

47-18 The same day Notre Dame stopped Oklahoma's winning streak at 47, what did Ohio State do?

47-19 Who was the QB when Bob Ferguson scored four TDs against Michigan in 1961 and later became an assistant coach for Woody Hayes?

47-20 What year did Ohio State defeat Michigan to break their string of 42 home wins?

ANSWERS GROUP 47

47-1 375-104-20 (.772%)

47-2 "TRESSELBALL"

47-3 Woody Hayes

47-4 27-2

47-5 Bobby Mitchell and Ray Nitschke

47-6 "White Out" (Penn State), "Black Out" (Purdue) and "Gold Out" (Iowa)

47-7 "Beanie" Wells, 222 yards

47-8 James Laurinaitis, Ohio State (2006); Glenn Dorsey, LSU (2007)

47-9 Beat O.J. Simpson USC, 1968; loss to Jim Plunkett Stanford, 1970

47-10 Wes Fesler

47-11 The Archie Griffin Award, given by the Touchdown Club of Columbus

47-12 Bob Atha (Indiana 1981), Mike Nugent (NCS 2004), Josh Huston (Texas 2006)

47-13 Chris "Beanie" Wells

47-14 Bill Willis, because of his speed and pursuit, while a Cleveland Brown

47-15 Dr. Warren Amling

47-16 Four undefeated (1954, 1961, 1968, 1973) and five one-loss seasons (1957, 1958, 1969, 1970, 1975)

47-17 NO hotel, it was a CONVENT!

47-18 Upset Iowa 17-13, won a trip to the Rose Bowl Game

47-19 QB John Mummey, #25

47-20 November 22, 1975, 21-14, on a Ray Griffin game winning interception

QUESTIONS **GROUP 48**

48-1 Which Ohio State head coach holds the record for most wins against Michigan?

48-2 Through 2007, when was the last time Ohio State won back-to-back outright Big Ten Championships?

48-3 Which Ohio State sports publication boasts the slogan "For the Buckeye fan that needs to know more?"

48-4 What is "The Glenn?"

48-5 Who were the other two key hires (nationally) when Jim Tressel was hired at Ohio State?

48-6 **T or F** LB Spielman and LB Laurinaitis have both been Butkus Award Finalists twice.

48-7 Which Buckeye quarterback flew 61 air missions during World War II?

48-8 In 2007, Head Coach Jim Tressel was a finalist for 1-A "Coach of the Year." Who won?

48-9 The worst snow storm since 1913 swept into Columbus for the great "Snow Bowl" Game in 1950. How many official inches of snow fell?

48-10 Who was a head coach at Wittenberg for 11 years and an assistant for 33 years at OSU?

48-11 Which OSU defensive coordinator became the head coach at Michigan State in 2007?

48-12 Who set the record, at the time, for the most rushing yards at 1,142 in a single season?

48-13 Which Hall of Fame member "flipped the coin" for the 2006 Ohio State-Michigan Game?

48-14 Name the four Buckeye running backs who have won the Maxwell Trophy for the nation's most outstanding offensive player.

48-15 How many years did two-time All-American LB Randy Gradishar play for the Denver Broncos?

48-16 How many times did Coach Earle Bruce win Ohio High School Coach of the Year?

48-17 Before the Heisman Memorial Trophy started in 1935, which two Buckeye players would have probably won the honor?

48-18 Who played tailback in the single-wing and QB in the T-formation in the same year?

48-19 How many straight State of Ohio High School Football Championships did Coach Paul Brown produce?

48-20 How many athletic directors has Ohio State had since 1912?

ANSWERS GROUP 48

48-1 Head Coach Woody Hayes with 16 WINS!

48-2 1954-1955

48-3 *Buckeye Sport Bulletin*

48-4 Another sure-handed catch by WR Terry Glenn

48-5 Pete Carroll (USC) and Bob Stoops (Oklahoma)

48-6 True

48-7 1945, QB Robin Priday

48-8 Head Coach Ron Zook, University of Illinois

48-9 Officially 9 inches, with more to come on Sunday!

48-10 College Football Hall of Fame Coach Ernie Godrey

48-11 Mark Dantonio, he did a great job at Ohio State for three years

48-12 John Brockington, 1970

48-13 Paul Warfield, Ohio State #1, BEAT #2 Michigan 42-39

48-14 1995 "Hop" Cassady, 1961 Bob Ferguson, 1976 Archie Griffin, 1995 Eddie George

48-15 10 years, 1974-1983, 7 Pro Bowls

48-16 Three times

48-17 "Chic" Harley and Wes Fesler

48-18 Les Horvath, 1944, and won the Heisman Memorial Trophy Award

48-19 Six State of Ohio High School and four High School National Champions 1935-1940 (58-1-1)

48-20 Eight: St. John, Larkins, Weaver, Hindman, Bay, Jones, Geiger and Smith

QUESTIONS GROUP 49

49-1 Who caught a 39-yard pass, with 39 seconds left on the clock to beat Pittsburgh in the 1983 Fiesta Bowl 28-23?

49-2 What two Big Ten stadiums are named after their home state?

49-3 How many players from the first OSU National Championship team were All-Americans?

49-4 In what year was the point value for a safety changed from one point to two points?

49-5 In what game in 2007 did the Ohio State Buckeyes tie Michigan's record of 19 straight conference victories?

49-6 Which Buckeye is a director on the National Football Foundation?

49-7 Who was Vic Janowicz's head coach the year he won the Heisman Memorial Trophy?

49-8 Who was the other African-American to FB Marion Motley on the Cleveland Browns?

49-9 How many outright Big Ten Championships did Head Coach John Cooper win in his 12-year career at Ohio State?

49-10 Who was the first Buckeye to catch five touchdown passes in an NFL game?

49-11 Who was nicknamed "Tree" by Woody for all the buckeye leaf awards on his helmet?

49-12 What five pro teams did QB Mike Tomczak play for from 1985 to 2000?

49-13 New England Patriots great linebacker Mike Vrabel played how many years as a back-up for the Pittsburgh Steelers?

49-14 **T or F** LSU was ranked No. 1 twice in 2007 and lost both times in triple overtime.

49-15 In what game did Jim Huston block a punt, intercept a pass and run both back scoring two touchdowns?

49-16 How many years had Ohio State played football before joining the Western Conference (later the Big Ten) in 1913?

49-17 Who was known for his "Pop-Block?"

49-18 Which famous U.S. humorist and cartoonist from Columbus, Ohio went to Columbus East High School with "Chic" Harley?

49-19 **T or F** Ohio State has walked off the field, thereby losing 1-0.

49-20 Name the three OSU players and the head coach who are in the Rose Bowl Hall of Fame.

ANSWERS GROUP 49

49-1   Thad Jemison, pass thrown by Mike Tomczak

49-2   Ohio Stadium (The Ohio State University); Michigan Stadium (University of Michigan)

49-3   Five: Csuri, Fekete, Houston, Sarringhaus and Shaw

49-4   1884

49-5   Penn State, broken the next week to 20 with the win against the Wisconsin Badgers

49-6   Archie Griffin

49-7   Wes Fesler, Woody Hayes coached Vic Janowicz his senior year in 1951

49-8   Bill Willis, a walk-on in 1945

49-9   None, shared titles in 1993, 1996 and 1998

49-10 Bob Shaw, 1950, with the Chicago Cardinals

49-11 Ted Provost, Safety, 1967-1969

49-12 Chicago Bears, Green Bay Packers, Cleveland Browns, Pittsburgh Steelers, Detroit Lions

49-13 Four years, 1997-2000

49-14 True: they are the only two-loss team to play in the BCS National Championship

49-15 Purdue 1958, winning 14-0

49-16 24 seasons, Ohio State started in 1890

49-17 Bill Willis, because of his quickness and leg strength

49-18 James Thurber

49-19 True: a game against Penn State in 1912 for excessive rough play!

49-20 "Curly" Morrison, Rex Kern, Archie Griffin and Head Coach Woody Hayes

QUESTIONS GROUP 50

50-1 Who was the first winner of the Chic Harley Award presented to the "College Player of the Year?"

50-2 Who is known as "The Senator?"

50-3 Who caught three touchdown passes in Ohio State's 500th game in the "Shoe" vs. NW?

50-4 Who was the first All-American quarterback to play for Head Coach Woody Hayes?

50-5 What year (season) was the "tied" game eliminated in Division 1-A football?

50-6 When was the only time the band has altered the famous "Script Ohio" formation?

50-7 How wide is a football field?

50-8 Which players had been one of the four finalists from Ohio State for the Butkus Award?

50-9 What was Head Coach John Cooper's bowl game record?

50-10 What year did RB Robert Smith lead the NFL in rushing with 1,521 yards?

50-11 Which Buckeye QB, as a running back in the Super Bowl, holds the record for the highest per-carry rushing average?

50-12 Who was known as "Ramblin' Rex?"

50-13 What did Coach Jim Tressel provide his players for Christmas presents in 2007?

50-14 *The Sporting News* (January 14, 2008) named which two Buckeyes as leading candidates for the 2008 Heisman Memorial Trophy?

50-15 Which Ohio State QB has thrown the most interceptions against Michigan?

50-16 What was the now-famous Buckeye cheer in regard to the USC Trojans in the 1980 Rose Bowl Game? *(It might show up again in the 2008 regular season game.)*

50-17 How many two-time AP All-Americans did Ohio State produce during 1969-1975?

50-18 **T or F** Archie Griffin won all sectionals both years that he won the Heisman Trophy.

50-19 Which Buckeye has the most all-purpose yards against the University of Michigan?

50-20 Which two-time All-American QB played in the first NCAA Basketball Tournament, with the Buckeyes losing to Oregon 46-33?

ANSWERS GROUP 50

50-1   Howard "Hopalong" Cassady, #40, 1955, by the Touchdown Club of Columbus

50-2   Head Coach Jim Tressel because of his composure and diplomatic style

50-3   Brian Robiskie

50-4   Rex Kern, #10, 1969

50-5   1996

50-6   1949, spelling "Chic" for a tribute to "Chic" Harley

50-7   160 feet wide x 120 yards long (including the end zones)

50-8   Chris Spielman, Andy Katzenmoyer, A.J. Hawk and James Laurinaitis

50-9   4-7 in 13 seasons

50-10 2000, with the Minnesota Vikings

50-11 Tom Matte, Baltimore Colts against the NY Jets, 1969 (10.5) 11 carries for 116 yards

50-12 QB Rex Kern, #10, 1968-1970

50-13 Motivational DVD about the "trashing" of the Buckeyes

50-14 LB James Laurinaitis and RB Chris Wells

50-15 Rex Kern, 4 interceptions, 1969, in a famous upset 24-12 by Bo

50-16 "Lubricate the Trojans"

50-17 Five players: Tatum, Stillwagon, Hicks, Gradishar and Griffin

50-18 False: Archie Griffin lost the Far West Sectional in 1975 to Chuck Muncie

50-19 RB Carlos Snow, 252 yards, 1988

50-20 QB Don Scott, 1938-1939 team

QUESTIONS **GROUP 51**

51-1   Who was the first Buckeye to play in three Rose Bowl games;
        1970, 1972 and 1973?

51-2   Which Buckeye linebacker was part of the NFL Denver Broncos
        "Orange Crush?"

51-3   What was Ohio State's record after its 500th game in Ohio
        Stadium?

51-4   As of 2007, how many times has Ohio State lost their
        season opener?

51-5   What was the first type of football called?

51-6   If we titled four eras as follows: Pre-World War II Era (1880-
        1940), World War II Era (1941-1945), Golden Era (1946-1965),
        and Modern Era (1966-2007), what might we be discussing?

51-7   **T or F**   Ohio State has the largest athletic budget in the
        United States.

51-8   What is the record for straight pass completions in a game?

51-9   Who was Ohio State's first African-American two-time
        All-American?

51-10   What was the most famous "Mass Momentum" play in football?

51-11   Which Ohio State head coach was the "Father of the Modern
        Offense?"

51-12   What year did Knute Rockne of Notre Dame want to replace
        retired Head Coach John Wilce at Ohio State?

51-13   Which Buckeye was *The Sporting News* AFL All-League Tackle
        eight straight years from 1962-1969?

51-14   Which Heisman Memorial Trophy winner was a coach for the
        minor league baseball team, The Columbus (Ohio) Clippers?

51-15   In 1992, who was honored as "Ohio State's Greatest Athlete of the
        Last Fifty Years?"

51-16   Who attempted the most field goals against Michigan in a game?

51-17   Which Ohio State head coach had Heisman Trophy winners over a
        25-year period?

51-18   Who was the last non African-American RB to gain 1,000 yards
        in a season?

51-19   Which Buckeye was a nine-time All-Pro selection, a "Hog" with
        the Washington Redskins and a Super Bowl winner?

51-20   Which one of Woody's tight ends was elected Mayor of Columbus,
        Ohio?

ANSWERS GROUP 51

51-1   Tackle John Hicks

51-2   LB Randy Gradishar

51-3   376-104-20 — a .772% winning percentage

51-4   ONLY 12 times out of 118 so far!

51-5   "Watermelon," it was approximately 21″ long and 25″ around. This was before passing was allowed!

51-6   The Evolution of the College Football Program, a fun collectible

51-7   True: $109 million plus, supporting 36 varsity teams

51-8   12: tied by Mrukowski (1961), Tomczak (1983), Karsatos (1985), Krenzel (2002), Boeckman (2007)

51-9   Bill Willis, 1943-1944

51-10   "The Flying Wedge," outlawed in the early 1900s

51-11   Paul Brown, 1941-1943 at Ohio State

51-12   Following the 1928 season!

51-13   Jim Tyrer

51-14   Howard "Hopalong" Cassady

51-15   1950 Heisman Memorial Trophy winner Vic Janowicz

51-16   Vlade Janakievski, 5 attempts, 1977

51-17   Woody Hayes, 1950-1975, Janowicz to Griffin, "Hop" was in the middle

51-18   RB Jeff Logan, 1,248 yards, 1976

51-19   Tackle Jim Lachey

51-20   Greg Lashutka, Mayor of Columbus Ohio, 1992-2000

QUESTIONS GROUP 52

52-1   Name the five teams in the top ten who all lost on the same weekend, moving Ohio State closer to the top in 2007?

52-2   The rule to make 10 yards in four plays was adopted in what year?

52-3   When did the "new" buckeye leaf insignia for the Bandsmen, designed by Milton Caniff, debut?

52-4   Who was the first Buckeye Heisman Memorial Trophy winner to play against another Big Ten Heisman Memorial Trophy winner?

52-5   Which Ohio State head coach played high school QB for Harry Stuhldreher, one of the famous Notre Dame "Four Horsemen?"

52-6   What is a hybrid of strong safety and linebacker?

52-7   Who is the only member of the College Football Hall of Fame to start in an NCAA Final Four game?

52-8   Who was the *Sports Illustrated* NFL Offensive Rookie of the Year in 2002?

52-9   Which Buckeye scored the first two-point conversion in NFL football history?

52-10   T or F   Ohio State finished first in all four defensive categories in 2007.

52-11   Who won Ohio State's 500th game at home in the "Shoe" against Wisconsin on October 23, 1948?

52-12   T or F   The same day Ohio State BEAT Michigan 50-14 in 1968, O.J. Simpson set the college rushing record.

52-13   T or F   Freshman QB Art Schlicter established an all-time single season record (at the time) for total offense in the Gator Bowl.

52-14   Which Buckeye kicked the longest field goal against Michigan?

52-15   Which Heisman Memorial Trophy winner, in his first game, came off the bench and scored three touchdowns against Indiana?

52-16   Which coach, a former Ohio State player, was known as the first coach to study game film?

52-17   Who was "The Big Kat?"

52-18   Which two Buckeyes have been two-time Fiesta Bowl MVPs?

52-19   Who is considered to be the top offensive lineman in the history of college football?

52-20   What All-American Buckeye RB was in the famous "Lite Beer" commercials?

ANSWERS GROUP 52

52-1   West Virginia, Oklahoma, Texas, Rutgers and Florida...all losing on September 29, 2007

52-2   1912, prior to that year it was 5 yards in 3 plays

52-3   During ceremonies at the "Snow Bowl" game, November 26, 1950

52-4   "Hop" Cassady vs. Alan "The Horse" Ameche, Wisconsin, 1954, Buckeyes won 31-14

52-5   Paul Brown at Washington High School, Massillon, Ohio

52-6   "Roverback"

52-7   All-American Warren Amling

52-8   LeCharles Bentley, New Orleans Saints Guard

52-9   Tom Tupa, with the Cleveland Browns against the Cincinnati Bengals, 1994

52-10   False: three categories only—passing, total and scoring; they finished third against the rush

52-11   Ohio State in a FANTASTIC 34-32 Victory!

52-12   True: but O.J. Simpson and the USC Trojans would lose a month later in the Rose Bowl Game to the National Champs, the Ohio State Buckeyes

52-13   True: game lost though to the Clemson Tigers, Woody's last game!

52-14   Tim Williams, 50 yards, 1991

52-15   Howard "Hopalong" Cassady, #40

52-16   Sid Gillman

52-17   1997 Butkus Award winner, LB Andy Katzenmoyer

52-18   QB Craig Krenzel, LB A.J. Hawk

52-19   Orlando Pace

52-20   Matt Snell

QUESTIONS GROUP 53

53-1   From 1968 to 1978, what did Ohio State accomplish in 11 seasons?

53-2   How many Big Ten titles did Michigan win in Woody's first 18 seasons at Ohio State?

53-3   What was Woody's record coaching against the Fighting Illini in14 seasons in Memorial Stadium?

53-4   What kind of "cocktails" did Woody serve after every game?

53-5   Ohio State equaled what record in 1954 (which had stood since 1913) with the University of Chicago?

53-6   Name the five Heisman Memorial Trophy winners who played on the field at Central High School in Columbus, Ohio?

53-7   Who was Archie Griffin's offensive backfield coach?

53-8   The same day Woody Hayes resigned, what did basketball Coach Eldon Miller do?

53-9   Which Buckeye opened holes for NFL Hall of Fame running back #32, Jim Brown, for the Cleveland Browns?

53-10 Who led Ohio State in tackles for three consecutive seasons between 1990 and 1992?

53-11 In the history of the "Horseshoe," since 1922, how many games have ended in a tie?

53-12 Ohio State started three seniors in the 2008 BCS Championship Game against LSU. How many seniors started for LSU?

53-13 How many straight points did LSU score after falling behind 10-0 in the 2008 BCS Championship Game?

53-14 Which three years have Ohio State vs. Michigan been undefeated-untied since 1935?

53-15 How many native sons of Ohio have won the Heisman Memorial Trophy?

53-16 Which Ohio State Buckeye kicker tied or broke 22 school records?

53-17 Which two Ohio State Heisman Memorial Trophy winners have been on a Super Bowl losing team?

53-18 T or F   Ohio State and Michigan both have the same total number of Bowl Game appearances.

53-19 How many Ohio State Athletic Conference Championships has Ohio State won?

53-20 All-time, what conference(s) does Ohio State have a losing record against, if any?

ANSWERS GROUP 53

53-1   9 Big Ten Titles, 2 National Championships, 2 Heisman Trophy winners

53-2   1 title in 1964

53-3   13-1, 1 loss in 1966

53-4   Orange juice...what else would you think it was?

53-5   7 league winning games when they BEAT Michigan 21-7

53-6   "Hop" Cassady, Les Horvath, Archie Griffin, Joe Belino and Roger Staubach

53-7   Mickey Jackson

53-8   Upset #1 ranked Duke 90-84 in overtime

53-9   Left Tackle Dick Schafrath

53-10 LB Steve Tovar, two-time All-American

53-11 20; and that will always be the record unless they switch back to tied ball games

53-12 23

53-13 31 straight points, winning 38-24

53-14 1970, 1973 and 2006

53-15 10; second only to the State of California with 14 (through 2007)

53-16 Mike Nugent, Lou Groza Award winner, 2004

53-17 Archie Griffin (Cincinnati Bengals) and Eddie George (Tennessee Titans)

53-18 True: through 2007-08 Michigan's record is 19-20; Ohio State 18-21 (Rose Bowl 6-7)

53-19 Two: 1906 (8-1-0) and 1912 (6-3-0) before joining the Western Conference (Big Ten)

53-20 Only 1 Conference: Southeastern Conference (SEC) 7-11-2

QUESTIONS **GROUP 54**

54-1 Which of Woody's National Championship teams lost its opener to TCU 18-14?

54-2 What year was it when uniform numbers were required on both the front and back of the player's jersey?

54-3 Who holds the record for the most interceptions in a game as a Buckeye?

54-4 Which Buckeye was a member of the Chicago Bears defensive team on the Super Bowl XX team in 1985?

54-5 **T or F** QB Kirk Herbstreit (1989-1993) never beat Michigan.

54-6 How many starters did Head Coach Paul Brown have returning for his 1942 team?

54-7 Who won the MVP Award in post-season games, The East-West Shrine and Hula Bowl?

54-8 **T or F** "Home Field Advantage" does not apply to the Ohio State vs. Michigan series.

54-9 Who was the first "true" Big Ten Quarterback to win the Heisman Memorial Trophy?

54-10 Which Buckeye is tied for the record for the longest fumble return in the NFL?

54-11 Before the 2007-08 season, when was the last time Ohio State played in the Rose Bowl?

54-12 How many times has Ohio State ever had 50 points scored against them?

54-13 Through 2007, who was the last opponent Ohio State shut-out at home in the "Shoe?"

54-14 What head coach holds the record through the 2007-08 season for the most points scored in a season?

54-15 How many net offensive yards did Michigan have in the 2007 game?

54-16 The 2007 loss to the Fighting Illini, broke what record?

54-17 How many field goals did Ohio State have blocked in the 2007-08 season?

54-18 Who is the smallest Heisman Memorial Trophy winner in the Modern Era, post-1950?

54-19 Who threw the key block on Play Pass 21 for QB Art Schlicter to score the winning TD upsetting Michigan 14-9 in 1981?

54-20 Who holds the record for the most rushing TDs in a career and total career TDs in Ohio high school football?

ANSWERS GROUP 54

54-1   1957
54-2   1937
54-3   "Chic" Harley against Michigan with four in 1919
54-4   Shaun Gayle
54-5   True: he never won a game, but Ohio State tied them 13-13 in 1992
54-6   Three, but they went 9-1 and won Ohio State's first National Championship
54-7   Vic Janowicz, 1950
54-8   False: home team – 52 victories, visitors – 46 wins
54-9   QB Troy Smith, #10, 2006
54-10 Jack Tatum, 104 yards, tied with Aeneas Williams
54-11 12 seasons ago —1997, beating Arizona State 20-17
54-12 6 times, only twice in the 1900s; 3 times OSU was shut-out!
54-13 The Minnesota Gophers, 44-0, on October 28, 2006
54-14 Head Coach John Cooper, position #1 (475 points) and #2 (455 points)
54-15 91 net yards, only 14 yards in the second half
54-16 Ohio State's and the Big Ten Conference record for consecutive wins at 20
54-17 Five. OUCH! Very unusual for the Buckeyes!
54-18 HB Howard "Hopalong" Cassady, #40, 1955
54-19 FB Vaughn Broadnax
54-20 Hubert Bobo, 132 total TDs, 118 yards rushing at Chauncey-Chauncey, Dover, Ohio 1953-56

QUESTIONS GROUP 55

55-1   What year did the NCAA start to keep official college football statistics?

55-2   **T or F** "The Best Damn Band in the Land" performed at half-time during the "Snow Bowl" game against Michigan in 1950.

55-3   Who called Head Coach Woody Hayes "A great competitor?"

55-4   How do "Meechigan" fans spell Columbus, Ohio?

55-5   Which Buckeye team scored the most points against a Duffy Daugherty's Michigan State Spartans team?

55-6   When was the last time (through 2007) Ohio State lost to an in-state team?

55-7   Which Ohio State Heisman Memorial Trophy winner had a two-position designation?

55-8   Who was the 1970 National Defensive Player of the Year?

55-9   Who wrote the first *Official Football Rules Book* (later called a "Guide") and in what year was it written?

55-10 Which major bowl game was discontinued in 1987, after 30 years?

55-11 What Kick-off Classic Game was played in Columbus, Ohio?

55-12 **T or F** Head Coaches Woody Hayes and John Cooper both had two seasons at .500 or below winning percentage.

55-13 Has Ohio State played all three of the service academies—Army, Navy and Air Force?

55-14 What is the longest running All-Star Bowl Game through the 2007-08 season?

55-15 How many times has Ohio State won four consecutive games against Michigan?

55-16 Since 1935, how many times has the Big Ten Football Championship been decided by the Ohio State-Michigan game?

55-17 What was the "Miracle in Michigan?"

55-18 Who said, "There is nothing that can make you feel better after losing this game?"

55-19 Which Ohio State team lost its first three games at home in "The Shoe" since 1922?

55-20 Name the two coaches and five players in the Pro Football Hall of Fame through 2008 from The Ohio State University.

ANSWERS GROUP 55

55-1 1937

55-2 True: the now famous photo shows the band doing the Hula Dancer Formation

55-3 Woody's close friend, Glenn "Bo" Schembechler

55-4 COWLUMBUS, AHIA

55-5 1969 team, 54 points

55-6 1921 to Oberlin 7-6 (173-48-15 all-time record)

55-7 Les Horvath, #22, QB/HB

55-8 Jack Tatum

55-9 Walter Camp "Father of American Football," 1885

55-10 The Blue Bonnet Bowl, Houston, Texas; Ohio State never played in this Bowl

55-11 Eddie Robinson Classic, August 28, 1997, Ohio State 24-Wyoming 10

55-12 True: Woody 1959 (3-5-1) and 1966 (4-5-0); Cooper 1988 (4-6-1) and 1999 (6-6-0)

55-13 NO, but vs. Navy (3-0), vs. Air Force (0-1), and we have not yet played Army

55-14 East-West Shrine Classic (83 years); Blue-Gray All-Star (64); Senior Bowl (58)

55-15 Three times! The last being 2007

55-16 23 times

55-17 2007 Appalachian State's UPSET of Mighty Michigan 34-32

55-18 Lloyd Carr, University of Michigan Head Football Coach

55-19 1967 Buckeyes

55-20 Coaches Paul Brown, Sid Gillman, players Lou Groza, Dante Lavelli, Jim Parker, Paul Warfield and Bill Willis

QUESTIONS GROUP 56

56-1 Which former player developed the famous "Zone Blitz?"

56-2 What is the "Toledo Cannon?"

56-3 Who holds the Ohio State record for starting the most games?

56-4 What was the league called that Bill Willis joined in 1946 with the Cleveland, Ohio team coached by former Ohio State Head Coach Paul Brown?

56-5 When was the first season Ohio State had two quarterbacks throw for over 1,000 yards?

56-6 Which Buckeye was the first ever to rush for 1,000 yards in each of his first three seasons in the NFL?

56-7 How old was Woody Hayes when he resigned?

56-8 Who set the record for the most tackles in a BCS Championship Game?

56-9 What is the "Ring of Honor" at The Ohio State University?

56-10 T or F The Home Depot's number 1 selling collegiate paint scheme in its Team Colors Program is Ohio State's scarlet and gray.

56-11 The city of Chicago had their "Artist Charity Cows." What does Ohio State have that is similar?

56-12 Who was the first Heisman Memorial Trophy winner to play both pro baseball and pro football?

56-13 Who is the only Ohio State player to ever win Ohio's High School "Mr. Football" twice?

56-14 Which Buckeye receiver has the most yards receiving in a single game against Michigan?

56-15 Which Big Ten team has the most Bowl Game victories?

56-16 How many 10-game (or more) winning seasons has Ohio State had through 2007?

56-17 What sporting goods company was famous for writing *The Official Football Guides*, starting in 1896?

56-18 Who was the only Heisman Trophy winner who did not play the previous season?

56-19 Head Coach Woody Hayes needed 18 seasons to get five top five finishes. How many seasons did it take Head Coach Jim Tressel?

56-20 Which Ohio State RB holds the Ohio high school record for most yards gained in a game?

ANSWERS GROUP 56

56-1   Dick LeBeau, also known as the "Fire Zone"

56-2   A symbolic cannon to honor the Ohio-Michigan land dispute over Toledo, Ohio

56-3   Tyson Walter, 49 games

56-4   All-American Football Conference

56-5   1996, Joe Germain with 1,193 yards and Stanley Jackson with 1,298 yards

56-6   John Brockington with the Green Bay Packers

56-7   65 years old, on Saturday, December 30, 1978

56-8   LB James Laurinaitis, 18 tackles vs. LSU, 2008

56-9   The retired player's jersey on "C" Deck in the Horseshoe

56-10   True: Michigan is third, Notre Dame is fifth

56-11   Artistic charity event, "Buckeye Brutuses"

56-12   Vic Janowicz, pro baseball with Pittsburgh Pirates and pro football with the Washington Redskins

56-13   Robert Smith (1988-1989)

56-14   David Boston, 217 yards, 1998

56-15   Penn State 26-12-2; Michigan 19-20-0; Ohio State 18-21-0

56-16   17

56-17   Spadling's until about 1946

56-18   QB/HB #22 Les Horvath, The Ohio State University, 1944

56-19   7 years

56-20   Bob Ferguson, 529 yards, Troy, Ohio vs. Dayton Kiser on September 14, 1956

QUESTIONS GROUP 57

57-1   **T or F**   Bill Wills was not allowed to play against the white players of the Miami Seahawks in 1945.

57-2   How many of John Cooper's recruited players earned All-American Honors at OSU?

57-3   Which two players won the Big Ten Offensive Lineman of the Year from 1993-1996?

57-4   What year did Ohio State have three players in the top six positions of Heisman Memorial Trophy voting?

57-5   Which OSU quarterback has the most pass completions against Michigan?

57-6   **T or F**   Ohio State has had different consecutive Bowl Game appearances of 15-10-8 year spans.

57-7   How many times was QB Todd Boeckman intercepted in the loss to Illinois in 2007?

57-8   Who was the new head coach to replace Michigan's Lloyd Carr in 2008?

57-9   Which two-way Heisman Trophy winner never had a pass completed on him while playing defensive back at Ohio State?

57-10   What were "Bee Hives," "Dog Ears," and "Flat Tops?"

57-11   Ohio State was 3 for 13 on 3rd downs against LSU in the BCS Championship Game. What were LSU's stats on 3rd downs?

57-12   In 2008, which two OSU players were nominated but did not receive enough votes (yet) to be inducted into the Pro Football Hall of Fame?

57-13   Numbering the players' jerseys was recommended in what year? In what year was it mandatory for visiting teams to wear white jerseys?

57-14   How many total tackles did James Laurinaitis have in 13 games in the 2007-08 season?

57-15   How many shut-outs did Ohio State's defensive team have in 2007?

57-16   How many rushes and yards did RB Chris Wells have against Michigan on November 17, 2007?

57-17   What was punter A.J. Trapasso's punting average against LSU in the BCS Championship Game?

57-18   When Ohio State entered the Red Zone in 2007, what was their percentage to score?

57-19   What season(s) did Ohio State win a National Championship with at least one loss?

57-20   **T or F**   Every bowl opponent of OSU's (when winning the National Championship) was from the PAC 10 Conference.

ANSWERS GROUP 57

57-1 True: the next year the Miami Seahawks were gone!

57-2 21 All-American Players, 1 Heisman Trophy Winner – Eddie George

57-3 Korey Stringer (1993-1994) and Orlando Pace (1995-1996)

57-4 John Hicks, Archie Griffin and Randy Gradishar in 1973

57-5 QB Troy Smith, #10, 29 completions, 2006

57-6 True: 15 (1972-1986), 10 (1989-1998), 8 (2000-20XX)

57-7 Three times, his worst game of the year!

57-8 Rich Rodriquez, Michigan's 18th Head Football Coach

57-9 Howard "Hopalong" Cassady, #40, 1995 Heisman Memorial Trophy Winner

57-10 The original leather-heads (helmets): Bee Hives 1900-1905, Dog Ears 1920s, Flat Tops 1910

57-11 11 for 18!

57-12 LB Randy Gradishar and WR Chris Carter

57-13 Recommended in 1915. In 1937 rules required 6" Arabic numeral on front and 10" Arabic numeral on back. 1983 visiting team wore white jerseys.

57-14 51 solo, 70 assist for a total of 121, 5 sacks, 2 interceptions, 1 fumble recovery

57-15 Zero. Akron scored 2 points; Kent State 3, Michigan 3

57-16 39 rushes for 222 yards in a 14-3 victory

57-17 50.0 yards

57-18 41 out of 47 (87.2%), opponents 19 of 23 (82.6%)

57-19 1942 (9-1-0) and 1957 (9-1-0)

57-20 False: 1954-57-68 Pac 10; 2002 Big East, Miami; no bowl opponent in 1942 or 1947

QUESTIONS GROUP 58

58-1   **T or F**   As of 1950, Vic Janowicz was only the third junior to win the Heisman Memorial Trophy.

58-2   Who kicked 22/28 field goals, 44/45 extra points, for 110 total points in a season?

58-3   Which Ohio State head coach qualified for a Rhodes Scholarship?

58-4   Name the three Buckeyes who have won the Walter Camp Award for the Best Player in College Football?

58-5   Which Buckeye was a member of the famous Minnesota Vikings "Purple People Eaters?"

58-6   How many Ohio State head coaches did not BEAT Michigan in their Ohio State career?

58-7   Which Ohio State player (selected by coaches) won the Big Ten Defensive Lineman of the Year Award, two years in a row?

58-8   The 1955 AP Male Athlete of the Year was "Hop" Cassady. Who preceded him and who succeeded him?

58-9   Which former Buckeye defensive back was involved in the "Immaculate Reception" between the Oakland Raiders and the Pittsburgh Steelers?

58-10   Where were the sites of the Great Lakes and Aviation Bowl games?

58-11   Which Buckeye Heisman Trophy winner set the record for winning percentage with 86.7% of the first place votes cast?

58-12   Which Ohio high school has the most State of Ohio Football Championships?

58-13   In what four Rose Bowls was Ohio State undefeated?

58-14   What year did platoon football return?

58-15   Has Ohio State or any other Big Ten team scored 500 points or more in a season?

58-16   How many years did Ohio State have a lowest single game of 10 total points when they won a National Championship?

58-17   Who kicked the winning field goal in the 1958 Rose Bowl Game of 24 yards to beat Oregon 10-7 and win a National Championship?

58-18   What one key play was the "Play of the Year" for the 1957 Buckeyes to win nine straight?

58-19   What has been the largest crowd in the 102,329 seat capacity of Ohio Stadium?

58-20   Who will be most likely to become Ohio State's ninth, three-time All-American in 2008?

ANSWERS GROUP 58

58-1   True: Archie Griffin was the next Ohio State junior to win a Heisman Memorial Trophy

58-2   John Huston, 2005

58-3   Paul Brown

58-4   1974-75, Archie Griffin (2x); 1995, Eddie George; 2006, Troy Smith

58-5   Jim Marshall

58-6   10 coaches, 1897-1912 and 1946-1950

58-7   Mike Vrabel, 1995-1996

58-8   1954 Willie Mays; 1956 Mickey Mantle

58-9   Jack Tatum, 1972

58-10   Great Lakes Bowl in Cleveland, Ohio for only two years, 1947-1948 and Aviation Bowl in Dayton, Ohio in 1961

58-11   QB Troy Smith, #10, 2006

58-12   Massillon Washington, 23 state titles

58-13   1950, 17-14 vs. California; 1955, 20-7 USC; 1958, 10-7 Oregon; 1969, 27-16 USC

58-14   1965, unlimited substitutions between periods and after a score

58-15   NO, has never been done in the Big Ten Conference

58-16   4 times: 1957, 10-7 vs. Oregon; 1961, 10-0 vs. Northwestern; 1970, 10-7 vs. Purdue; 2002, 10-6 vs. Purdue

58-17   Don Sutherin, he punted, place-kicked, played running back and defensive back

58-18   An 81-yard punt return (Don Dutherin), against Washington, a 35-7 win!

58-19   105,708 vs. Michigan on November 18, 2006; probably will be much higher in 2008!

58-20   LB James Laurinaitis

QUESTIONS GROUP 59

59-1 Which Buckeye player was an All-American at guard one year and then All-American at tackle the next year?

59-2 **T or F** Head Coach Jim Tressel is the only coach to win the Coach of the Year Award at two different schools for the American Football Coaches Association (AFCA).

59-3 Which Ohio State All-American, College Hall of Fame member, coached/developed 16 All-American linemen at Oklahoma University?

59-4 **T or F** Coach John W. Heisman, for whom the Heisman Memorial Trophy is named, beat Ohio State.

59-5 What year was the suspension helmet introduced to increase safety in the game?

59-6 Which two juniors from Ohio State have won the Heisman Memorial Trophy?

59-7 Which head coach started the "Jack Tatum Hit of the Week" Award?

59-8 As of the 2008 bowl games, which team has the current consecutive bowl appearance record?

59-9 What two FB wore/used the same "chin strap" in the Michigan game seven years apart?

59-10 The Big Ten Conference was also known by what other name?

59-11 How many times has Ohio State been out of the Top 10 in Decade Rankings since 1930?

59-12 How many current major bowl games exist today; which one is the oldest?

59-13 Through 2007, how many games has Ohio State scored 50 points or more?

59-14 Which coach holds the record for most points scored against the Buckeyes in a season?

59-15 What was Michigan Head Coach Lloyd Carr's record against the Ohio State Buckeyes?

59-16 **T or F** Between 1933 and 1940, the Ohio State/Michigan loser was always shut-out.

59-17 What happened each year against Michigan when Ohio State was 9-0-1 (1993), 11-0 (1995) and 10-0 (1996)?

59-18 Where was Ohio State ranked in the 2007 Big Ten Conference pre-season?

59-19 What year was the rule for freshman eligibility restored?

59-20 How many yards did Chris Wells rush for in 2007?

ANSWERS GROUP 59

59-1   Warren Amling, 1945-1946

59-2   True: ACFA American Football Coaches Association

59-3   Gomer Jones

59-4   True: In 1894 while coaching at Buchtel College (now Akron)

59-5   1939

59-6   Vic Janowicz, 1950 and Archie Griffin, 1974

59-7   Jim Tressel, 2001

59-8   Michigan with 33 games, starting in 1975; Ohio State is tied in 8th position with 8 games

59-9   FB Bob Ferguson, 1961 and FB Jim Otis, 1968. Both scored four touchdowns!

59-10 Western Conference and/or Intercollegiate Conference of Faculty Representatives (ICFR), 1896-1986

59-11 1 time, 1980-1989

59-12 32 Bowl Games; Rose Bowl 94 years as of 2007-08 season

59-13 70 times! 32 shut-outs

59-14 Head Coach John Cooper, 339 points, ranks 1, 2, 3, 7, 8, 9 in Top Ten

59-15 6-7 career vs. The Buckeyes; 1-6 against Coach Jim Tressel

59-16 True: the teams split 4-4

59-17 Ohio State LOST!

59-18 3rd behind Michigan and Penn State

59-19 1972

59-20 1,609 yards (123.8 avg/game) in 13 games, leading with 15 touchdowns

QUESTIONS GROUP 60

60-1 The week Les Horvath won the Heisman Memorial Trophy, what did golfer Byron Nelson get for winning the San Francisco Open?

60-2 In 1950, how many points was Vic Janowicz responsible for in the 83-21 win over Iowa?

60-3 Who is Ohio State's only Rhodes Scholar?

60-4 What "special team skill" did Linebacker A.J. Hawk possess?

60-5 Who holds the record for the most PAT by a Buckeye against the Michigan Wolverines?

60-6 **T or F** From 1972-1976, Bo and Woody won the Big Ten Coach of the Year four out of five seasons.

60-7 Which stadium has hosted the most Heisman Memorial Trophy winners and runner-ups?

60-8 Who played for Coach Paul Brown at OSU and then led the Baltimore Colts to a win in Super Bowl V as a first year head coach?

60-9 Who was Ohio State's best punting quarterback?

60-10 What year did college football statistics become official?

60-11 What four years did Jim Tressel win a NCAA-1-AA National Championship at Youngstown State?

60-12 **T or F** Ohio State played at the Ohio State Fair.

60-13 Which head coach had the greatest spread between points scored for and against the Ohio State Buckeyes in a single season?

60-14 **T or F** Through 2007, three head coaches are tied with 10+ wins a season at five each.

60-15 Which three head coaches had undefeated and untied seasons with a minimum of nine games?

60-16 How many sacks did Vernon Gholston have on Michigan's QB Chad Henne in 2007?

60-17 What happened to the Buckeyes and the Wolverines the week before the 2007 Ohio State-Michigan game?

60-18 **T or F** At one time there was a rule against concealing the ball underneath a player's jersey.

60-19 **T or F** Through 2007 (72 years of AP Polls), Ohio State is first with the most No. 1 rankings.

60-20 Name the five "greatest traditions" of Ohio State Football!

ANSWERS GROUP 60

60-1 War Bonds ($2,666.00) the date was December 5, 1944

60-2 46 points

60-3 Mike Lanese, 1985

60-4 Punting! Averaged 40 yards a kick in high school

60-5 Van Raaphorst, 6 in 1961

60-6 True: Bo, 1972 and 1976; Woody, 1973 and 1975

60-7 "The Horseshoe," Ohio Stadium, "The Shoe"

60-8 Don McCafferty

60-9 Tom Tupa, 1987, 63 punts / 47.0 yards average

60-10 1937

60-11 1991-1993-1994-1997

60-12 True: vs. Wittenberg, September 7, 1894, losing 0-6

60-13 Woody Hayes, 1973, points "for" 413, points "against" 64; 349 point difference

60-14 True: Woody Hayes, John Cooper and Jim Tressel

60-15 Widdoes (1944), 9-0; Hayes (1954 and 1968), 10-0; Tressel (2002), 14-0

60-16 Three sacks! 20-3 Buckeye Victory!

60-17 They both LOST! Ohio State to Illinois 28-21 and Michigan to Wisconsin 37-21

60-18 True: 1911, it is just not for comedy movies

60-19 False: Ohio State is third with 93, behind Notre Dame and Oklahoma tied for first with 95 times at No. 1

60-20 *There is no right or wrong answer!* Here are my favorites, please add your choices: "The Shoe," Woody, The Band (Script Ohio and the ramp entrance), The Michigan Game, Tailgating, Rivalry...

QUESTIONS GROUP 61   *National Championship*

61-1 **T or F** Ohio State was the first Big Ten team to win an AP National Championship.

61-2 How many years did Woody Hayes coach at Ohio State, before winning his first title?

61-3 How many times have the Buckeyes and USC met in a bowl game and the winner was later voted No. 1?

61-4 Counting the final poll, how many weeks has Ohio State been a weekly AP No. 1 and then was later the National Champion?

61-5 Name the seasons in which the National Champion Buckeyes were also in the final top 10 in rushing stats?

61-6 How many times has a National Championship Game gone into overtime?

61-7 In what years that Ohio State won the title, did a Buckeye finish in the top five balloting for the Heisman Memorial Trophy?

61-8 How many times has OSU played an SEC team during the season and later was voted No. 1?

61-9 Four NCAA Bowl Subdivision teams (1A) have won a total of seven National Championships; one is Ohio State, name the other three.

61-10 Name the alma maters of each of the Buckeye head coaches that have won the National Championship.

61-11 How many times has an alumnus of Ohio State, regardless of division or association, won a National Championship title?

61-12 Of the seasons of National Championships, what is Ohio State's composite record?

61-13 What was OSU's highest offensive scoring average when it won a title and what was the lowest defensive scoring average?

61-14 How many shut-outs has OSU's defense recorded in National Championship seasons?

61-15 What is the Buckeyes record vs. teams ranked in the AP final poll during a championship season?

61-16 How many times has Ohio State been the AP's Pre-Season No.1?

61-17 OSU has entered a bowl game ranked No. 1 how many times and how many games have they won?

61-18 In what year did Ohio State receive its initial UP/UPI final appearance?

61-19 Counting polls from pre-season, final regular season and final post-bowl polls, how many times, total, has Ohio State been No. 1?

61-20 What was Ohio State's highest AP ranking before winning the 1942 AP National Championship?

ANSWERS ■ GROUP 61

National
Championship

61-1 False: Minnesota was the first in 1936

61-2 Four seasons, started in 1951 and in 1954 won his first title

61-3 4 times, each team winning twice; OSU in 1954 (20-7) and 1968 (27-16); USC in 1972 (42-17) and 1974 (18-17)

61-4 18 weeks

61-5 1942, 3rd (283.3); 1961, 4th (271.9); 1968, 3rd (306.4); and 1970, 3rd (306.8); Ohio State's ground game has been an OSU trademark!

61-6 Just once, when Ohio State beat Miami of Florida in 2002

61-7 Two times: 1954, Howard "Hop" Cassady was third; 1961, Bob Ferguson was second

61-8 None

61-9 Alabama, Oklahoma and USC

61-10 Paul Brown, 1942 (Miami of Ohio, 1930); Woody Hayes, 1954, 1957, 1961, 1968 and 1970 (Denison, 1935); and Jim Tressel, 2002 (Baldwin-Wallace, Ohio, 1975)

61-11 Five times: Bill Bell, Florida A & M (HBCU), 1939-42; Rudy Hubbard, Florida A & M (HBCU), 1977 and (NCAA 1AA and HBCU), 1978; Sam Willaman led the Buckeyes to a title in 1933.

61-12 70-3-1: 1942 (9-1); 1954 (10-0); 1957 (9-1); 1961 (8-0-1); 1968 (10-0); 1970 (10-1); and 2002 (14-0)

61-13 Scoring average: 1942 (33.7 points) and defensive scoring average: 1954 (7.5 points)

61-14 Nine times!

61-15 18-0-0

61-16 None. The Buckeyes were ranked No. 2 twice, in 1998 and 2006

61-17 Four times and winning none

61-18 1957, when it was named the National Championship

61-19 16 times…7-2-2 respectfully (FYI, second to Oklahoma's 20)

61-20 13th in 1937 and 1941

Ohio State Fight Songs

BUCKEYE BATTLE CRY

In old Ohio there's a team
That's known thru-out the land;
Eleven warriors, brave and bold,
Whose fame will ever stand.
And when the ball goes over,
Our cheers will reach the sky,
Ohio Field will hear again
The Buckeye Battle Cry!
Drive! Drive on down the field,
Men of the scarlet and gray;
Don't let them through that line,
We've got to win this game today,
Come on, Ohio!
Smash through to victory.
We cheer you as you go!
Our honor defend
So we'll fight to the end for O-hi-o

ACROSS THE FIELD

Fight the team across the field,
Show them Ohio's here
Set the earth reverberating with a mighty cheer
Rah! Rah! Rah!
Hit them hard and see how they fall,
Never let that team get the ball,
Hail! Hail! The gang's all here,
So let's win that old conference now.

Ohio State Alma Mater

CARMEN OHIO

Oh! Come let's sing Ohio's praise,
And songs to Alma Mater raise;
While out hearts rebounding thrill,
With joy which death alone can still.
Summer's heat or Winter's cold,
The seasons pass, the years will roll;
Time and change will surely show
How firm thy friendship O-hi-o.
These jolly days of priceless worth,
By far the gladdest days of earth,
Soon will pass and we not know,
How dearly we love O-hi-o.
We should strive to keep the name,
Of fair repute and spotless fame,
So, in college halls we'll grow,
To love the better, O-hi-o.
Tho' age may dim our mem'ry's store,
We'll think of happy days of yore,
True to friend and frank to foe,
As sturdy sons of O-hi-o.
If on seas of care we roll,
'Neath blackened sky, o'er barren shoal,
Tho 'ts of thee bid darkness go,
Dear Alma Mater O-hi-o.

OHIO
The Heart of It All

State Capital:	Columbus (1816)
State Bird:	Cardinal
State Tree:	Ohio Buckeye *(Aesculus glabra)*
State Flower:	Scarlet Carnation
State Wildflower:	White Trillium
State Song:	*Beautiful Ohio*
State Rock Song:	*Hang on Sloopy*
State Flag:	Swallowtail Pennant Design (1901)
State Beverage:	Tomato Juice
State Fossil:	Isotelus
State Gemstone:	Flint
State Groundhog:	"Buckeye Chuck"
State Insect:	Ladybug
State Mammal:	White-tailed Deer
State Reptile:	Black Racer
State Water Borders:	Lake Erie (North), Ohio River (South)
State Area:	40,948 square miles; 44,825 including Lake Erie
State Size:	34th
State Dimensions:	225 East to West; 215 North to South
State Population:	7th, 11.5 million +
State Name:	"Goodriver" from Iroquois Indians
State Nickname:	The Buckeye State
State Other Name:	AHIA or O-HI-O
State Motto:	With God, all things are possible
Statehood:	March 1, 1803, 17th state to enter Union
State Abbreviation:	OH
Highest Elevation:	Campbell Hill, 1,550 ft., 43rd
Lowest Elevation:	Ohio River, 433 ft., 36th
Mean Elevation:	850 ft.
Largest City:	Columbus
Number of Counties:	88
Interstate Mileage:	1,326 miles
Scenic Byways:	24, www.ohiobyways.com

Go Bucks!™ BEAT MICHIGAN®

OHIO STADIUM
The Horseshoe, The Shoe, The House Harley Built

Year Built:	1922
Previous Field:	Ohio Field on North High Street by 17th & Woodruff Avenues
Architect:	Howard Dwight Smith
Conceptualized and Designed:	1918
Original Project Name:	Athletic Field and Stadium
Officially Named:	Ohio Stadium, April 25, 1921
Design Awards:	Gold Medal for Smith from American Institute of Architects
Ground Breaking Ceremony:	August 3, 1921
Construction Company:	E.H. Latham Company of Columbus, Ohio
Construction Material:	Concrete, however some wanted it to be done in brick
Athletic Director:	Lynn W. St. John (St. John Arena named in his honor)
Visionary:	Prof. Thomas French (French Field House named in his honor)
Original Cost:	$1,341,017.00 Contract Price
Stadium Completion Date:	October 1, 1922; Actual Price $1,488,168.00
Fundraising Campaign Name:	Stadium Week, October 18-23, 1920
Rotunda:	Dome designed after the Pantheon in Rome, Italy
Track:	Originally cinder, later the Jesse Owens Track, and then removed during renovation in 2001
First Game:	Ohio Wesleyan, October 7, 1922 Ohio State 5-0 Win
Dedication Game:	Michigan, October 21, 1922, a loss—or should I say—an upset
Original Seating Capacity:	66,210
Present Seating Capacity:	102,329; 4th largest in the United States
Seats in "A" Deck:	27,192
Seats in "AA" Deck:	8,318

OHIO STADIUM CONTINUED

Seats in "B: Deck:	19,718
Seats in "C" Deck:	30,878
Seats in "D" Deck:	2,459
Seats in 81 Hospitality Suites:	1,062
Seats in the South Stands:	17,248
Club Seats:	2,625
Largest Crowd:	The Michigan Game, November 18, 2006, 105,708 Fans
Total Attendance Since 1922:	39 million and growing! Never lower than 4th national since 1949
Conference:	The Big Ten
Pro Team Stadium:	Ohio Glory of the American Football League (now defunct)
Playing Surface:	Field Turf
Renovation:	1999-2001
Re-Dedication:	Akron, 2001
Honors & Recognition:	National Park Service; National Register of Historic Places, March 22, 1974; The Cathedral of College Football
Address:	411 Woody Hayes Drive Columbus, Ohio 43210
Operator:	The Ohio State University Department of Athletics
Bordering River:	The Olentangy River
Field Lights:	None. Usually, temporarily installed *for night games and events*
Flag Pole Height:	162 feet total (16 feet in the ground)
Scoreboard:	Installed in 1984 at a cost of $2.1 million. New scoreboard in 2001 renovation
MLS:	The Columbus Crew was 30-18 in Ohio Stadium, 1996-1999
Practice Facilities:	Woody Hayes Athletic Center
Players Entrance:	"Tunnel of Pride," started with Michigan game in 1994, a 22-6 win!

OHIO STADIUM CONTINUED

Victory Bell:	Bell rung with each victory by the Alpha Phi Omega Fraternity since 1954. Bell weight is 2,420 pounds and is located in the southeast corner tower of the Ohio Stadium.
Student Cheering Section:	Block "O", started in 1938 by Cheerleader, Clancy Isaac. It is the largest student organization at Ohio State and is located in the South Stands.
Buckeye Grove:	Since 1934, a buckeye tree is planted along with a plaque to honor Ohio State All-Americans in the "Buckeye Grove" located just southwest of the Ohio Stadium.
Latitude & Longitude of 50-Yard Line:	40° North; 83° West (approximately)
Total Square Feet of A Concourse:	536,850 square feet
Ohio Stadium Circumference:	2,892 feet
Length of Ohio Stadium:	919 feet
Width of Ohio Stadium:	679 feet
Height of Ohio Stadium Out-build from Grade Level:	136 feet, 7 inches
Height of Press Box Roof from Grade Level:	168 feet, 10 inches
Renovated Field Lowered:	14 feet, 6 inches and removed running track
Square Footage of Ohio Stadium Build Pad:	624,001 square feet
Total Number of Acres:	14.5 acres
Total Playing Field Acres:	1.6 acres
Scoreboard Height and Width:	42 feet high, 158 feet, 2 inches wide
Video Screen Height and Width:	30 feet high, 90 feet wide
Number of Men's Fixtures:	437
Number of Women's Fixtures:	723
Family Restrooms:	24
Point-of-Sale Concessions:	194

Source: Stadium Facts OSU

Popular Ohio State Football Websites

www.aroundtheoval.com

www.brutusreport.com

www.buckeye50.com

www.buckeyebanter.com

www.buckeyebuzz.com

www.buckeyecommentary.com

www.buckeyextra.com

www.buckeyefansonly.com

www.buckeyegrove.com

www.buckeyelane.com

www.buckeyelegends.com

www.buckeyeplanet.com

www.buckeyesports.com

www.buckeyes247.com

www.bucknuts.com

www.coachtressel.com

www.collegesports-fans.com

www.columbusdispatch.com

www.cstv.com/teams.osu

www.elevenwarriors.com

www.menofthescarletandgray.com

www.ohiostatebuckeyes.com

www.ohiostate.scout.com

www.osumensvo.com

www.tbdbitl.osu.edu

www.theozone.net

College Football Websites

All-American Football Association	www.aafootballfoundation.com
American Football Coaches Association	www.afca.com
College Football Hall of Fame	www.collegefootball.org
Football Bowl Association	www.footballbowlassociation.com
Football Writers Association of America	www.footballwriters.com
National College Football Awards Association	www.ncfaa.com
National Football Foundation	www.footballfoundation.com
NCAA Football	www.ncaafootball.com

Division 1-A Conference Websites

Atlantic Coast (ACC)	www.theacc.com
Big East	www.bigeast.org
Big Ten	www.bigten.org
Big 12	www.big12sports.com
Conference USA	www.conferenceusa.com
Mid-American (MAC)	www.mac-sports.com
Mountain West	www.themwc.com
Pacific-10 (PAC 10)	www.pac-10.org
Southeastern (SEC)	www.secsports.com
Sun Belt	www.sunbeltsports.org
Western Athletic (WAC)	www.wacsports.com

Football Bowl Websites

Bowl Championship Series (BCS)	www.bcsfootball.org
Valero Alamo Bowl	www.alamobowl.com
Bell Helicopter Armed Forces Bowl	www.armedforcesbowl.com
Capital One Bowl	www.fcsports.com
Champs Sports Bowl	www.fcsports.com
Chick-fil-a Bowl	www.chick-fil-abowl.com
AT&T Cotton Bowl Classic	www.attcottonbowl.com
Emerald Bowl	www.emeraldbowl.org
Tostitos Fiesta Bowl	www.fiestabowl.org
Gator Bowl Classic	www.gatorbowl.com
GMAC Bowl	www.gmacbowl.com
Sheraton Hawaii Bowl	www.sheratonhawaiibowl.com
Pacific Life Holiday Bowl	www.pacificlifeholidaybowl.com
Roady's Humanitarian Bowl	www.humanitarianbowl.org
PetroSun Independence Bowl	www.independencebowl.org
Insight Bowl	www.insightbowl.org
International Bowl	www.internationalbowl.org
Pioneer Las Vegas Bowl	www.lvbowl.com
AutoZone Liberty Bowl	www.libertybowl.org
Meineke Car Care Bowl	www.meinekecarcarebowl.com
Motor City Bowl	www.motorcitybowl.com
Gaylord Hotels Music City Bowl	www.musiccitybowl.com
New Mexico Bowl	www.newmexicobowl.com
R+L Carriers New Orleans Bowl	www.neworleansbowl.com
FedEx Orange Bowl	www.orangebowl.org
Outback Bowl	www.outbackbowl.com
Papajohns.com Bowl	www.papajohnsbowl.com
San Diego County Credit Union Poinsettia Bowl	www.pointsettiabowl.net
The Rose Bowl Game	www.tournamentofroses.com
Allstate Sugar Bowl	www.allstatesugarbowl.com
Brut Sun Bowl	www.sunbowl.org
Texas Bowl	www.texasbowl.net

All-Star Football Bowl Game Websites

East-West Shrine Game	www.shrinegame.com
Hula Bowl All-Star Football Classic	www.hulabowlhawaii.com
Under Armour Senior Bowl	www.seniorbowl.com

Buckeye Bowl History

SEASON	BOWL	SCORE
2007	BCS Title Game	LSU 38, Ohio State 24
2006	BCS Title Game	Florida 41, Ohio State 14
2005	Fiesta	Ohio State 34, Notre Dame 20
2004	Alamo	Ohio State 33, Oklahoma State 7
2003	Fiesta	Ohio State 35, Kansas State 28
2002	BCS Title Game	Ohio State 31, Miami 24 (2 OT)
2001	Outback	South Carolina 31, Ohio State 28
2000	Outback	South Carolina 24, Ohio State 7
1998	Sugar	Ohio State 24, Texas A&M 14
1997	Sugar	Florida State 31, Ohio State 14
1996	Rose	Ohio State 20, Arizona State 17
1995	Citrus	Tennessee 20, Ohio State 14
1994	Citrus	Alabama 24, Ohio State 17
1993	Holiday	Ohio State 28, BYU 21
1992	Citrus	Georgia 21, Ohio State 14
1991	Hall of Fame	Syracuse 24, Ohio State 17
1990	Liberty	Air Force 23, Ohio State 11
1989	Hall of Fame	Auburn 31, Ohio State 14

BUCKEYE BOWL HISTORY CONTINUED

SEASON	BOWL	SCORE
1986	Cotton	Ohio State 28, Texas A&M 12
1985	Citrus	Ohio State 10, BYU 7
1984	Rose	USC 20, Ohio State 17
1983	Fiesta	Ohio State 28, Pittsburgh 23
1982	Holiday	Ohio State 47, BYU 17
1981	Liberty	Ohio State 31, Navy 28
1980	Fiesta	Penn State 31, Ohio State 19
1979	Rose	USC 17, Ohio State 16
1978	Gator	Clemson 17, Ohio State 15
1977	Sugar	Alabama 35, Ohio State 6
1976	Orange	Ohio State 27, Colorado 10
1975	Rose	UCLA 23, Ohio State 10
1974	Rose	USC 18, Ohio State 17
1973	Rose	Ohio State 42, USC 21
1972	Rose	USC 42, Ohio State 17
1970	Rose	Stanford 27, Ohio State 17
1968	Rose	Ohio State 27, USC 16
1957	Rose	Ohio State 10, Oregon 7
1954	Rose	Ohio State 20, USC 7
1949	Rose	Ohio State 17, California 14
1920	Rose	California 28, Ohio State 0

DIVISION 1-A
Teams, Stadiums, Nicknames and Mascots

TEAM	STADIUM	NICKNAME	MASCOT
ACC Conference			
Boston College	Alumni Stadium	Eagles	Baldwin the Eagle
Clemson	Memorial Stadium	Tigers	Tiger
Duke	Wallace Wade Stadium	Blue Devils	The Blue Devil
Florida State	Doak Campbell Stadium	Seminoles	Chief Osceola
Georgia Tech	Dodd Stadium	Yellow Jackets	Buzz
Maryland	Byrd Stadium	Terrapins	Testudo
Miami (FL)	Orange Bowl	Hurricanes	Ibis
North Carolina	Kenan Stadium	Tar Heels	Rameses
N.C. State	Carter Finley Stadium	Wolfpack	Mr. & Mrs. Wuf
Virginia	Scott Stadium	Cavaliers	Cavman
Virginia Tech	Lane Stadium	Hokies	Hokie Bird
Wake Forest	BB&T Field	Demon Deacons	Demon Deacon
BIG EAST Conference			
Cincinnati	Nippert Stadium	Bearcats	The Bearcat
Connecticut	Rentschler Field	Huskies	Husky
Louisville	Cardinal Stadium	Cardinals	Cardinal
Pittsburgh	Heinz Field	Panthers	ROC the Panther
Rutgers	Rutgers Stadium	Scarlet Knights	Scarlet Knight
Syracuse	Carrier Dome	Orangeman	Otto the Orange
USF	Raymond James Stadium	Bulls	Rocky the Bull
West Virginia	Mountaineer Field	Mountaineers	The Mountaineer

TEAMS, STADIUMS, NICKNAMES, MASCOTS CONTINUED

TEAM	STADIUM	NICKNAME	MASCOT
BIG TEN Conference			
Illinois	Memorial Stadium	Fighting Illini	Chief Illiniwek
Indiana	Memorial Stadium	Hoosiers	
Iowa	Kinnick Stadium	Hawkeyes	Herky the Hawk
Michigan	Michigan Stadium	Wolverines	
Michigan State	Spartan Stadium	Spartans	Sparty
Minnesota	Metrodome	Golden Gophers	Goldy the Gopher
Northwestern	Ryan Field	Wildcats	Willie the Wildcat
Ohio State	Ohio Stadium	Buckeyes	Brutus Buckeye
Penn State	Beaver Stadium	Nittany Lions	The Nittany Lion
Purdue	Ross Ade Stadium	Boilermakers	Boilermaker Special
Wisconsin	Camp Randall Stadium	Badgers	Bucky Badger

TEAM	STADIUM	NICKNAME	MASCOT
BIG 12 Conference			
Baylor	Floyd Casey Stadium	Bears	Bruiser
Colorado	Folsom Field	Golden Buffaloes	Ralphie
Iowa State	Trice Stadium	Cyclones	Cy
Kansas	Memorial Stadium	Jayhawks	Baby Jay (Big Jay)
Kansas State	KSU Stadium	Wildcats	Willie the Wildcat
Missouri	Faurot Field	Tigers	Truman the Tiger
Nebraska	Memorial Stadium	Cornhuskers	Herbie Husker
Oklahoma	Memorial Stadium	Sooners	Sooner Schooner
Oklahoma State	Pickens Stadium	Cowboys	Pistol Pete
Texas	Royal Memorial Stadium	Longhorns	Bevo (Hookem')
Texas A & M	Kyle Field	Aggies	Reveille
Texas Tech	Jones AT&T Stadium	Red Raiders	Raider Red

TEAMS, STADIUMS, NICKNAMES, MASCOTS CONTINUED

TEAM	STADIUM	NICKNAME	MASCOT
CONFERENCE USA			
East Carolina	Dowdy Ficklen Stadium	Pirates	Pee Dee the Pirate
Houston	Robertson Stadium	Cougars	Shasta
Marshall	Joan Edwards Stadium	Thundering Herd	Marco
Memphis	Liberty Bowl	Tigers	Pouncer (Tom II)
Rice	Rice Stadium	Owls	Sammy the Owl
SMU	Gerald Ford Stadium	Mustangs	Peruna
Southern Miss	Roberts Stadium	Golden Eagles	Seymour d' Campus
Tulane	Superdome	Green Wave	Riptide the Pelican
Tulsa	Skelly Stadium	Golden Hurricanes	Captain Cane
UAB	Legion Field	Blazers	Dragon
UCF	Citrus Bowl	Golden Knights	Knightro
UTEP	Sun Bowl	Miners	Paydirt Pete

MID-AMERICAN (MAC) Conference

TEAM	STADIUM	NICKNAME	MASCOT
Akron	Rubber Bowl	Zips	Zippy the Kangaroo
Ball State	Ball State Stadium	Cardinals	Charlie Cardinal
Bowling Green	Doyt Perry Stadium	Falcons	Freddie Falcon
Buffalo	UB Stadium	Bulls	Victor E. Bull
Central Michigan	Kelly Shorts Stadium	Chippewas	Flying C
Eastern Michigan	Rynearson Stadium	Eagles	Swoop
Kent State	Dix Stadium	Golden Flashes	Flash
Miami (Ohio)	Fred Yager Stadium	Redhawks	Swoop the Red Hawk
Northern Illinois	Huskie Stadium	Huskies	Victor E. Huskie
Ohio University	Peden Stadium	Bobcats	Rufus
Temple	Lincoln Financial Field	Owls	Owls
Toledo	Glass Bowl	Rockets	Rocky the Rocket
Western Michigan	Waldo Stadium	Broncos	Buster Bronco

TEAMS, STADIUMS, NICKNAMES, MASCOTS CONTINUED

TEAM	STADIUM	NICKNAME	MASCOT
MOUNTAIN WEST Conference			
Air Force	Falcon Stadium	Falcons	Fighting Falcon
BYU	LaVell Edwards Stadium	Cougars	Cosmo the Cougar
Colorado State	Hughes Stadium	Rams	Cam the Ram
New Mexico	University Stadium	Lobos	Lobo Louie
San Diego State	Qualcomm Stadium	Aztecs	Montezuma the Aztec
TCU	Amon Carter Stadium	Horned Frogs	Super Frog
UNLV	Sam Boyd Stadium	Running Rebels	Hey Reb
Utah	Rice Edwards Stadium	Utes	Swoop
Wyoming	War Memorial Stadium	Cowboys	Cowboy Joe
PAC-10 Conference			
Arizona	Arizona Stadium	Wildcats	Wilber Wildcat
Arizona State	Sun Devil Stadium	Sun Devils	Sparky
California	Memorial Stadium	Golden Bears	Oski
Oregon	Autzen Stadium	Ducks	Donald Duck
Oregon State	Reser Stadium	Beavers	Benny
Stanford	Stanford Stadium	Cardinals	The Stanford Tree
UCLA	Rose Bowl	Bruins	Bruin (Bear)
USC	LA Coliseum	Trojans	Traveler
Washington	Husky Stadium	Huskies	Harry
Washington State	Martin Stadium	Cougars	Butch T. Cougar

TEAMS, STADIUMS, NICKNAMES, MASCOTS CONTINUED

TEAM	STADIUM	NICKNAME	MASCOT
SEC Conference			
Alabama	Bryant Denny Stadium	Crimson Tide	Big AL
Arkansas	Razorback Stadium	Razorbacks	Big Red (Boss Hogg)
Auburn	John Hare Stadium	Tigers	Aubie (War Eagle VI)
Florida	Ben Hill Griffin Stadium	Gators	Albert E. Gator
Georgia	Sanford Stadium	Bulldogs	UGA
Kentucky	Commonwealth Stadium	Wildcats	The Wildcat
LSU	Tiger Stadium	Tigers	Mike the Tiger
Ole Miss	Vaught Hemingway	Rebels	Colonel Reb
Mississippi State	Scott Field	Bulldogs	Bully
South Carolina	Williams Brice Stadium	Gamecocks	Cocky
Tennessee	Neyland Stadium	Volunteers	Smokey
Vanderbilt	Vanderbilt Stadium	Commodores	Mr. C

TEAM	STADIUM	NICKNAME	MASCOT
SUN BELT Conference			
Arkansas State	Indian Stadium	Indians	(Mascot Review)
Florida Atlantic	Lockart Stadium	Owls	Owsley
Florida Intl.	FIU Stadium	Golden Panthers	Roary the Panther
Middle Tennessee	Floyd Stadium	Blue Raiders	Lightning
Louisiana-Lafayette	Cajun Field	Ragin Cajuns	Cayenne
Louisiana-Monroe	Malone Stadium	Indians	(Mascot Review)
North Texas	Fouts Field	Eagles	Scrappy
Troy	Movie Gallery Stadium	Trojans	Trojan

TEAMS, STADIUMS, NICKNAMES, MASCOTS CONTINUED

TEAM	STADIUM	NICKNAME	MASCOT
WAC Conference			
Boise State	Bronco Stadium	Broncos	Buster Bronco
Fresno State	Bulldog Stadium	Bulldogs	Bulldog
Hawaii	Aloha Stadium	Rainbows	Warriors
Idaho	Kibbie Dome	Vandals	Joe Vandel
Louisiana Tech	Joe Aillet Stadium	Bulldogs	Tech XIX
Nevada	Mackay Stadium	Wolf Pack	Wolfie
New Mexico State	Aggie Memorial Stadium	Aggies	Pistol Pete
San Jose State	Spartan Stadium	Spartans	Spartans
Utah State	Romney Stadium	Aggies	Big Blue
Independents			
Army	Michie Stadium	Black Knights	Black Jack
Navy	Memorial Stadium	Midshipmen	Bill the Goat
Notre Dame	Notre Dame Stadium	Fighting Irish	The Leprechaun
Western Kentucky	L.T. Smith Stadium	Hilltoppers	Big Red Toppers

National College Football Awards

CHUCK BEDNARIK AWARD
www.maxwellfootballclub.org
Nation's Best Defensive Player by the Maxwell Football Club

THE BILETNIKOFF AWARD
www.biletnikoffaward.com
Nation's Outstanding Receiver by the Tallahassee Quarterback Club Foundation

FRANK BROYLES AWARD
www.broylesaward.com
Assistant Coach of the Year by the Rotary Club of Little Rock

BUTKUS AWARD
www.butkusaward.org
Nation's Outstanding Linebacker by the DAC of Orlando

WALTER CAMP AWARD
www.waltercamp.org
Nation's Top Overall Player by the Walter Camp Foundation

DISNEY'S WIDE WORLD OF SPORTS SPIRIT AWARD
www.wdwpress.com/split
Most Inspirational Player or Team by Disney Sports Attractions

DRADDY TROPHY
www.footballfoundation.com
Nation's Top Collegiate Scholar-Athlete by the National Football Foundation

LOU GROZA AWARD
www.lougrozaaward.com
Nation's Top Place Kicker by the Palm Beach County Sports Commission

RAY GUY AWARD
www.augustasportscouncil.org
Nation's Top Punter by the Greater Augusta Sports Council

HEISMAN MEMORIAL TROPHY
www.heisman.com
Nation's Most Outstanding Player by the Heisman Trophy Trust

ROTARY LOMBARDI AWARD
www.rotarylombardiaward.com
Nation's Lineman of the Year by the Rotary Club of Houston

NATIONAL COLLEGE FOOTBALL AWARDS CONTINUED

JOHN MACKEY AWARD
www.johnmackeyaward.org
Nation's Top Tight End by the Nassau County Sports Commission

MAXWELL AWARD
www.maxwellfootballclub.org
Outstanding Player of the Year by the Maxwell Football Club

GEORGE MUNGER AWARD
www.maxwellfootballclub.org
Outstanding Coach of the Year by the Maxwell Football Club

BRONKO NAGURSKI TROPHY
www.touchdownclub.com
Outstanding Defensive Player by the FWAA Charlotte Touchdown Club

DAVEY O'BRIEN AWARD
www.daveyobrien.com
Nation's Best Quarterback by the Davey O'Brien Foundation

OUTLAND TROPHY
www.outlandtrophy.com
Best Interior Offensive or Defensive Lineman by the FWAA

RIMINGTON TROPHY
www.rimingtontrophy.com
Nation's Outstanding Center by the Boomer Esiason Foundation

EDDIE ROBINSON AWARD
www.eddierobinsonaward.com
Nation's Top Division 1-A Coach by the Tostitos Fiesta Bowl & the FWAA

JIM THORPE AWARD
www.jimthorpeassoc.org
Nation's Outstanding Defensive Back by the Jim Thorpe Association

DOAK WALKER
www.doakwalkeraward.com
Nation's Best Collegiate Running Back
by the Guaranty Bank SMU Athletic Forum

MAJOR OHIO STATE FOOTBALL AWARDS WINNERS
through 2007–08 Season

The Heisman Memorial Trophy
Outstanding Player of the Year

1944	#22	Les Horvath QB/HB
1950	#31	Vic Janowicz HB
1955	#40	Howard "Hopalong" Cassady HB
1974	#45	Archie Griffin RB
1975	#45	Archie Griffin RB
1995	#27	Eddie George RB
2006	#10	Troy Smith QB

Walter Camp Award
Player of the Year

1974	#45	Archie Griffin
1975	#45	Archie Griffin
1995	#27	Eddie George
2006	#10	Troy Smith

Rotary Lombardi Award
Best Lineman LM or Linebacker LB

1970	#68	Jim Stillwagon LB
1973	#74	John Hicks LM
1987	#36	Chris Spielman LB
1995	#75	Orlando Pace LM
1996	#75	Orlando Pace LM
2005	#47	A.J. Hawk LB

Outland Trophy
Best Inside Offensive Lineman IOL or Defensive Lineman DL

1956	#62	Jim Parker IOL
1970	#68	Jim Stillwagon DL
1973	#74	John Hicks IOL
1996	#75	Orlando Pace IOL

Doak Walker Award
Best Running Back

1995	#27	Eddie George

Ray Guy Award
Best Punter

2003	#21	B.J. Sander

Lou Groza Award
Best Placekicker

2004	#85	Mike Nugent

Jim Thorpe Award
Best Defensive Back

1998	#11	Antoine Winfield

Bronko Nagurski Trophy
Best All-Around Defensive Player

2006	#33	James Laurinaitis

Maxwell Award
Player of the Year

1955	#40	Howard "Hopalong" Cassady
1961	#46	Bob Ferguson
1975	#45	Archie Griffin
1995	#27	Eddie George

Davey O'Brien Award
Best Quarterback

2006	#10	Troy Smith

MAJOR OSU FOOTBALL AWARD WINNERS CONTINUED

Fred Biletnikoff Award
Best Wide Receiver
1995 #83 Terry Glenn

Dick Butkus Award
Best Linebacker
1997 #45 Andy Katzenmoyer
2007 #33 James Laurinaitis

Rimington Trophy
Best Center
2001 LeCharles Bentley

Wuerffel Trophy
Athletic & Academic Achievement
2006 #98 Joel Penton

Draddy Trophy
Academic Heisman
1995 #14 Bobby Hoying
2003 #16 Craig Krenzel

Walter Camp
Coach of the Year
1968 Wayne Woodrow "Woody" Hayes

Eddie Robinson Award
Coach of the Year
1957 Wayne Woodrow "Woody" Hayes
1968 Wayne Woodrow "Woody" Hayes
1975 Wayne Woodrow "Woody" Hayes
1979 Earle Bruce
2002 Jim Tressel

Paul 'Bear' Bryant
Coach of the Year Award
1957 Wayne Woodrow "Woody" Hayes
1968 Wayne Woodrow "Woody" Hayes
1975 Wayne Woodrow "Woody" Hayes
1979 Earle Bruce
2002 Jim Tressel

American Football Coaches
Coach of the Year
1944 Carroll Widdoes
1957 Wayne Woodrow "Woody" Hayes
1979 Earle Bruce
2002 Jim Tressel

Frank Broyles Award
Assistant Coach of the Year
2007 Jim Heacock,
       Defensive Coordinator

The MacArthur Trophy
Outstanding Team
1968 The Ohio State University
1970 The Ohio State University
2002 The Ohio State University

Grantland Rice Trophy
Division I-A National Champion
1957 The Ohio State Buckeyes
1968 The Ohio State Buckeyes
2002 The Ohio State Buckeyes

MAJOR OSU FOOTBALL AWARD WINNERS CONTINUED

College Football Hall of Fame

Players	Inducted
Warren Amling	1984
Howard Cassady	1979
Jim Daniell	1977
Bob Ferguson	1996
Wes Fesler	1954
Randy Gradishar	1998
Archie Griffin	1986
Chic Harley	1951
John Hicks	2001
Les Horvath	1969
Jim Huston	2006
Vic Janowicz	1976
Gomer Jones	1978
Rex Kern	2007
Jim Parker	1974
Jim Stillwagon	1991
Gaylord Stinchcomb	1973
Jack Tatum	2004
Aurealius Thomas	1989
Bill Willis	1971
Gust Zarnas	1975

Coaches	Inducted
Earle Bruce	2002
John Cooper	2008
Woody Hayes	1983
Howard Jones	1951
Francis Schmidt	1971
John Wilce	1954

Pro Football Hall of Fame
Players

Lou Groza	Tackle, Kicker
Dante Lavelli	End
Jim Parker	Guard-Tackle
Paul Warfield	Receiver
Bill Willis	Middle Guard

Coaches

Paul Brown	Browns, Bengals
Sid Gillman	Rams, Chargers, and Oilers

Retired Jersey Numbers

#45	Archie Griffin	(10-30-99)
#31	Vic Janowicz	(9-23-00)
#40	"Hop" Cassady	(11-18-00)
#22	Les Horvath	(10-6-01)
#27	Eddie George	(11-10-01)
#47	"Chic" Harley	(10-30-04)
#99	Bill Willis	(11-3-07)
	Woody Hayes	(9-10-05)

John Mackey Award*
Best Tight End

Chuck Bednarik Award*
Best Defenseman

John Unitas Golden Arm Award*
Best Senior Quarterback

George Munger Award*
Coach of the Year

Disney Spirit Award*
Most Inspirational Player or Team

*Awards not yet won by a Buckeye

OHIO STATE
FIRST TEAM ALL-AMERICANS

1914	Boyd Cherry	E
1916	Chic Harley	B
	Robert Karch	T
1917	Charles Bolen	E
	Harold Courtney	E
	Chic Harley	B
	Kelley VanDyne	C
1918	Clarence MacDonald	E
1919	Chic Harley	B
	Gaylord Stinchcomb	B
1920	Iolas Huffman	G
	Gaylord Stinchcomb	B
1921	Iolas Huffman	T
	Cyril Myers	E
1923	Harry Workman	QB
1924	Harold Cunningham	E
1925	Edwin Hess	G
1926	Edwin Hess	G
	Martin Karow	HB
	Leo Raskowski	T
1927	Leo Raskowski	T
1928	Wesley Fesler	E
1929	Wesley Fesler	E
1930	Wesley Fesler	E
	Lew Hinchman	HB
1931	Carl Cramer	QB
	Lew Hinchman	HB
1932	Joseph Gailus	G
	Sid Gillman	E
	Lew Hinchman	HB
	Ted Rosequist	T
1933	Joseph Gailus	G
1934	Regis Monahan	G
	Merle Wendt	E
1935	Gomer Jones	C
	Merle Wendt	E
1936	Charles Hamrick	T
	Inwood Smith	G
	Merle Wendt	E
1937	Carl Kaplanoff	T
	Jim McDonald	QB
	Ralph Wolf	C
	Gust Zarnas	G

1939	Vic Marino	G
	Esco Sarkkinen	E
	Donald Scott	HB
1940	Donald Scott	HB
1942	Robert Shaw	E
	Charles Csuri	T
	Lindell Houston	G
	Paul Sarringhaus	HB
	Gene Fekete	
1943	Bill Willis	T
1944	Les Horvath	QB/HB
	Jack Dugger	E
	Bill Willis	T
	William Hackett	G
1945	Warren Amling	G
	Ollie Cline	FB
	Russell Thomas	T
1946	Warren Amling	T
	Cecil Souders	E
1950	Victor Janowicz	HB
	Robert Momsen	T
	Robert McCullough	C
1952	Mike Takacs	G
1954	Dean Dugger	E
	Howard Cassady	HB
	Jim Reichenbach	G
1955	Howard Cassady	HB
	Jim Parker	G
1956	Jim Parker	G
1957	Aurealius Thomas	G
1958	James Houston	E
	Jim Marshall	T
	Bob White	FB
1959	Jim Houston	E
1960	Bob Ferguson	FB
1961	Bob Ferguson	FB
1964	Jim Davidson	T
	Ike Kelley	LB
	Arnie Chonko	DB
1965	Douglas Van Horn	G
	Ike Kelley	LB
1966	Ray Pryor	C

OHIO STATE FIRST TEAM ALL-AMERICANS CONTINUED

1968	David Foley	OT		1985	Thomas Johnson	LB
	Rufus Mayes	OT		1986	Cris Carter	SE
1969	Jim Stillwagon	G			Chris Spielman	LB
	Rex Kern	QB		1987	Chris Spielman	LB
	Jim Otis	FB			Tom Tupa	P
	Ted Provost	CB		1988	Jeff Uhlenhake	C
	Jack Tatum	CB		1991	Steve Tovar	LB
1970	Jim Stillwagon	MG		1992	Steve Tovar	LB
	John Brockington	FB		1993	Korey Stringer	OT
	Jack Tatum	CB			Dan Wilkinson	DT
	Mike Sensibaugh	S		1994	Korey Stringer	OT
	Tim Anderson	CB		1995	Eddie George	TB
	Jan White	TE			Terry Glenn	FL
1971	Tom DeLeone	C			Orlando Pace	OT
1972	John Hicks	OT			Mike Vrabel	DE
	Randy Gradishar	LB		1996	Orlando Pace	OT
1973	John Hicks	OT			Shawn Springs	CB
	Randy Gradishar	LB			Mike Vrabel	DE
	Archie Griffin	TB		1997	Andy Katzenmoyer	LB
	Van Ness DeCree	DE			Rob Murphy	OG
1974	Archie Griffin	TB			Antoine Winfield	CB
	Van Ness DeCree	DE		1998	David Boston	SE
	Kurt Schumacher	OT			Damon Moore	SS
	Pete Cusick	DT			Rob Murphy	OG
	Steve Myers	C			Antoine Winfield	CB
	Neal Colzie	CB		1999	Na'il Diggs	LB
	Tom Skladany	P		2000	Mike Doss	SS
1975	Archie Griffin	TB		2001	LeCharles Bentley	C
	Ted Smith	OG			Mike Doss	SS
	Tim Fox	S		2002	Mike Doss	SS
	Tom Skladany	P			Andy Groom	P
1976	Bob Brudzinski	DE			Mike Nugent	K
	Chris Ward	OT			Matt Wilhelm	LB
	Tom Skladany	P		2003	Will Allen	SS
1977	Chris Ward	OT			Will Smith	DE
	Aaron Brown	NG		2004	A.J. Hawk	LB
	Tom Cousineau	LB			Mike Nugent	K
	Ray Griffin	S			Ted Ginn Jr.	PR
1978	Tom Cousineau	LB		2005	A.J. Hawk	LB
1979	Ken Fritz	OG		2006	Troy Smith	QB
	Art Schlichter	QB		2006	Quinn Pitcock	DT
1982	Marcus Marek	LB			James Laurinaitis	LB
1984	James Lachey	OG		2007	James Laurinaitis	LB
	Keith Byars	TB				

Go Bucks!™ BEAT MICHIGAN.

BUCKEYE LEAF AWARD CRITERIA

ENTIRE TEAM

Goal	(all criteria in each row must be met to earn a Buckeye Leaf)	Awarded to
✹	Win – every team member will receive a Buckeye Leaf after a victory	Team
✹	Big Ten – every team member will receive an additional Buckeye Leaf for a Big Ten win	Team
✹	Win T.O. Margin	Team
✹	Winning Performance – each individual that meets the film grade standard as set by the staff receives a Buckeye Leaf • Offensive Lineman 80% • Defensive Lineman 80% • Tailback 90% • Fullback 85% • Linebacker 85% • Defensive Back 90% • Quarterback 85% • Wide Receiver 85%	Individual
✹	Big play in football game as designated by Coach Tressel	Individual

DEFENSIVE UNIT

Goal	(In each category if criteria is met, the entire defensive unit that played significantly will receive an award)	Awarded to
✹	Hold opponents to 13 points or less (if sufficient for an OSU victory)	Defensive Unit
✹	Defensive Score	Defensive Unit
✹	Five "3 and outs"	Defensive Unit
✹	Stop opponents in all sudden change situations	Defensive Unit
✹	Stop opponent inside their own 10-yard line so that Ohio State obtains the ball in "plus territory"	Defensive Unit
✹	Stop opponent in all two-minute situations	Defensive Unit
✹	Force three (3) turnovers	Defensive Unit

BUCKEYE LEAF AWARD CRITERIA CONTINUED

SPECIAL UNITS BUCKEYE LEAF CRITERIA

Goal	■ KICKOFF TEAM (all criteria in each row must be met to earn a Buckeye Leaf)	Awarded to
✲	Result inside 25-yard line every time No penalties No missed tackles 11 hustling in proper lanes	Kickoff Team
✲	Recover onside kick	Kickoff Team
✲	Cause fumble and recovery	Individual
✲	Tackle inside 20-yard line	Individual

Goal	■ PUNT TEAM (all criteria in each row must be met to earn a Buckeye Leaf)	Awarded to
✲	Net punt 35 yards No rushed or blocked punts No penalties No missed tackles 11 hustling in proper lanes	Punt Team
✲	Successful fake punt for 1st down	Punt Team
✲	Down punt inside 10-yard line	Punt Team
✲	Cause fumble/recovery	Individual

Goal	■ KICK-OFF RETURN TEAM (all criteria in each row must be met to earn a Buckeye Leaf)	Awarded to
✲	All returnable kicks past 25-yard line No fumbles No penalties Never lose an onside kick	Kick-Off Team
✲	Kick-off returned past 40-yard line	Kick-Off Team

Goal	■ RANGERS (all criteria in each row must be met to earn a Buckeye Leaf)	Awarded to
✲	Average 5 yards or more per return Catch in air all catchable punts No fumbles No penalties	Rangers
✲	Punt returned over 20 yards	Rangers
✲	Block or force a poor punt	Rangers

BUCKEYE LEAF AWARD CRITERIA CONTINUED

SPECIAL UNITS BUCKEYE LEAF CRITERIA

Goal	■ FIELD GOAL / EXTRA POINT TEAM (all criteria in each row must be met to earn a Buckeye Leaf)	Awarded to
✹	100% PAT success and 40-yard field goal or less 75% field goal success outside 40 yards No penalties 100% Mechanics No rushed or blocked kicks or penetration	FG / XP Team
✹	Successful fake field goal attempt	FG / XP Team
✹	45+ yard field goal	Individual

Goal	■ FIELD GOAL / EXTRA POINT BLOCK TEAM (all criteria in each row must be met to earn a Buckeye Leaf)	Awarded to
✹	Blocked attempt or pressure forcing miss	Block Team
✹	Preventing fake attempt	Block Team
✹	Score	Block Team

Source: The Ohio State University

ALL-TIME OHIO STATE COACHING RECORDS
through 2007–08 Season

COACH	YEARS	WON	LOST	TIED	PCT.	vs TSUN
Alexander S. Lilley	1890-1891	3	5	0	.375	
Jack Ryder	1892-95 & 98	22	22	2	.500	
Charles A. Hickey	1896	5	5	1	.500	
David F. Edwards	1897	1	7	1	.167	0-1-0
John B. Eckstorm	1899-1901	22	4	3	.810	0-1-1
Perry Hale	1902-1903	14	5	2	.714	0-2-0
E.R. Sweetland	1904-1905	14	7	2	.652	0-2-0
A.E. Hernstein	1906-1909	28	10	1	.731	0-4-0
Howard Jones	1910	6	1	3	.750	0-0-1
Harry Vaughn	1911	5	3	2	.600	0-1-0
John R. Richards	1912	6	3	0	.667	0-1-0
John W. Wilce	1913-1928	78	33	9	.688	4-7-0
Sam S. Willaman	1929-1933	26	10	5	.695	2-3-0
Francis A. Schmidt	1934-1940	39	16	1	.705	4-3-0
Paul E. Brown	1941-1943	18	8	1	.685	1-1-1
Carroll E. Widdoes	1944-1945	16	2	0	.889	1-1-0
Paul O. Bixler	1946	4	3	2	.556	0-1-0
Wesley E. Fesler	1947-1950	21	13	3	.608	0-3-1
Woody Hayes	1951-1978	205	61	10	.761	16-11-1
Earl Bruce	1979-1987	81	26	1	.755	5-4-0
John Cooper	1988-2000	111	43	4	.715	2-10-1
Jim Tressel	2001-2007	73	16	0	.820	6-1-0

COLLEGE FOOTBALL RIVALRIES

College football rivalries are one of the best things that come out of the college football experience. This page is just for fun! Rank your favorite rivalries; rank your Top 10, your Top 25, or rank them by conference…you decide. Make up your own critique for rankings, add some, or scratch some out…but have fun with it!

____ Ohio State vs. Michigan	____ Texas vs. Texas A&M
____ Auburn vs. Alabama	____ UCLA vs. USC
____ Harvard vs. Yale	____ Georgia vs. Georgia Tech
____ Indiana vs. Purdue	____ Texas vs. Oklahoma
____ Arizona vs. Arizona State	____ Florida State vs. Miami
____ Notre Dame vs. USC	____ Florida vs. Georgia
____ Nebraska vs. Oklahoma	____ Virginia vs. Virginia Tech
____ Minnesota vs. Wisconsin	____ Kansas vs. Missouri
____ Colorado vs. Colorado State	____ Auburn vs. Georgia
____ Florida vs. Florida State	____ Lafayette vs. Lehigh
____ Michigan vs. Michigan State	____ Notre Dame vs. Michigan
____ Alabama vs. Tennessee	____ Oregon vs. Oregon State
____ Clemson vs. South Carolina	____ Arkansas vs. LSU
____ Washington vs. Washington State	____ Miami vs. Florida
____ Mississippi State vs. Ole Miss	____ Citadel vs. V M I
____ William & Mary vs. Richmond	____ Iowa vs. Iowa State
____ Miami (OH) vs. Ohio University	____ California vs. Stanford
____ Oklahoma vs. Oklahoma State	____ Kentucky vs. Louisville
____ Nebraska vs. Kansas	____ Minnesota vs. Wisconsin
____ Pittsburgh vs. Penn State	____ Ohio State vs. Penn State
____ Kansas vs. Kansas State	____ Tennessee vs. Florida
____ Miami (OH) vs. Cincinnati	____ _____
____ Minnesota vs. Michigan	____ _____
____ Army vs. Navy	____ _____

BUCKEYE RECIPES

BUCKEYE CANDY

1 stick of butter
1 box powdered sugar
1-1/2 cups peanut butter
1 tsp. vanilla
1 pkg. (12 oz.) chocolate chips
1/2 stick paraffin

Soften butter and mix with sugar, peanut butter and vanilla until a smooth texture develops. Form into bite-size balls (the size of large shooting-type marbles). Let cool in refrigerator.

Melt chocolate and paraffin in a double boiler pan. When chocolate is melted, take a toothpick and stick into peanut ball and dip into the chocolate/paraffin mixture, leaving part of the top uncovered and place on waxed paper. This will take on the appearance of a buckeye. The toothpick hole may be touched up with chocolate.

Refrigerate and enjoy!

MAGOO'S BUCKEYE BISCUITS

(12-ounce) can biscuits
3 to 4 cups vegetable oil, for deep frying

Drop biscuits in hot oil for 2 to 3 minutes per side until golden brown. Drain on paper towels.

Serve with MAGOO's Buckeye Butter:
1 bottle of squeeze margarine
3/4 cup of Hershey's Chocolate syrup
1/2 cup of creamy peanut butter
1/2 cup honey, or to taste
1/4 cup brown sugar
1/2 tsp cinnamon

Open squeeze bottle and pour about 1/2 of the margarine in a bowl. Add chocolate syrup, peanut butter, honey, brown sugar and cinnamon. Place in microwave for about 20 seconds or until all ingredients are blended. Pour into a plastic squeeze bottle. Squeeze into hot biscuit with the pointed end of the bottle.

Eat and Yell, "Go Bucks!"

Ohio State Football Bibliography
from Mike McGuire's Football Book Collection

AFCA American Football Coaches Association
Football Coaching Strategies

Aryal, Aimee
"Brutus' Journey through the Buckeye State"
"Hello Brutus!"

Bruce, Earle
Buckeye Wisdom: Insight and Inspiration from Coach Earle Bruce
Earle: A Coach's Life

Brondfield, Jerry
Woody Hayes and the 100-Yard War

Buchanan, Andy
100 Things Buckeye Fans Should Know & Do Before They Die

Bynum, Mike (edited by)
Woody Hayes: The Man & His Dynasty

Cohen, Richard M. et al
The Ohio State Football Scrapbook

Collett, Ritter
The Story of OSU's Art Schlichter (Signed by Art Schlichter)

Conley, Bill
Buckeye Bumper CrOps

Cromartie, Bill
The Big One: Michigan vs. Ohio State: A Game-by-Game History of America's Greatest Football Rivalry

Curteich, John Hinde
Ohio State Tailgate Cookbook

Diles, Dave
ARCHIE (Signed by Archie Griffin)

Emmanuel, Greg
*The 100-Yard War: Inside the 100-Year-Old
Michigan–Ohio State Football Rivalry*

Epstein, Brad M.
Ohio State Buckeyes 1 2 3: My first counting book

Fowble, Amy
It's fun to be a Buckeye

Game Day
*Ohio State Football: The Greatest Games, Players, Coaches,
and Teams in the Glorious Tradition of Buckeye Football*

Greenberg, Steve
*Ohio State '68: All the Way to the Top. The Story of Ohio State's
Undefeated Run to the Undisputed 1968 National Football Championship*

I Remember Woody: Recollections of the Man They Called Coach Hayes

Game of My Life: Ohio State: Memorable Stories of Buckeye Football

Griffin, Archie (foreword by)
The Greatest Moments in Ohio State Football History

The Archie Griffin Story

Harper, William H.
*An Ohio State Man: Coach Esco Sarkkinen
Remembers OSU Football*

Hayes, Woody
Football at Ohio State (Scarce)

Hot Line to Victory

You Win with People

You Win with People, Updated with Three New Chapters

Homan, Marv & Hornung, Paul
Ohio State 100 Years of Football

Hooley, Bruce
Greatest Moments in Ohio State Football History

Hornung, Paul
Woody Hayes: A Reflection

Hunter, Bob
The Buckeyes: Ohio State Football

Johnson, Dick
Columbus Discovers Football [Ohio State Football]

Kaelin, Eric
Buckeye Glory Days: The Most Memorable Games of Ohio State Football

Kearney, Tom
Buckeyes Big Game Book

Keels, Paul (Signed)
Tales from the Buckeye Championship Season

Klein, Fredrick C.
For the Love of the Buckeyes

Levy, William V.
Three Yards and a Cloud of Dust: The Ohio State Football Story

McGuire, Mike
500 Ohio State Football Trivia Q & A
800 Ohio State Football Trivia Q & A
500 Heisman Football Trivia Q & A
1220 Ohio State Football Trivia Q & A

Menzer, Joe
Buckeye Madness: The Glorious, Tumultuous,
Behind-the-scenes Story of Ohio State Football

Ohio State University Dept. of Athletics
Annual Ohio State Football Media Guide

Park, Jack
Ohio State Football...the Great Tradition
Ohio State Football Encyclopedia
The Official Ohio State Football Encyclopedia
Ohio State Football Encyclopedia:
National Championship Limited Edition
Ohio State University Football Vault

Pennington, Joel (Signed)
The Ten Year War, Ten Classic Games Between Bo and Woody

Porentas, John
A Photo History of the New Era in Ohio State Football

Queen, Paul
Where is Brutus?

Quigley, Brendan Emmett
Ohio State Crossword Puzzle Book:
25 All-New Buckeye Football Trivia Puzzles

Rea, Mark
When Legends Were Made: Ohio State Buckeyes

Shade, Laurie
The Little Buckeye Book

Shapiro, Harvey
Class of 68: A Season to Remember

Sharpe, Wilton
Buckeye Madness: Great Eras in Ohio State Football

Skipton, Todd W.
A shot at a Rose, to the Bite of a Gator:
The '75-'78 Ohio State Football Saga

Snook, Jeff
Then Tress Said to Troy   The Best Ohio State Football Stories Ever Told
(with CD)

Snapp, Steve
Diary of an Unforgettable Season: 2006 Ohio State Buckeyes

Snypp, Wilbur
The Buckeyes: A Story of Ohio State Football

Steinberg, Donald
Expanding Your Horizons: Collegiate Football's Greatest Team
(Paul Brown, Ohio State Football)

The Ohio State University Marching Band
"Script Ohio: Evolution"

Thomson, Tom
All-Time History of the Battling Buckeyes: The Story of Ohio State Football 1890-1952. (1st Edition, Very Scarce)

Tressel, Jim
What It Means To Be a Buckeye
The Winners Manual: For the Game of Life

Vare, Robert
Buckeye: A Study of Coach Woody Hayes and the Ohio State Football Machine

Weigel, J. Timothy
The Buckeyes: Ohio State Football

White, Steve
One Game Season: Ohio State versus Michigan

Wolfe, Rich
For BUCKEYE FANS Only!

Purchase the in-print books from any one of the Ohio State Collegiate Team Logo Stores or National Book Store Chains in Columbus, Ohio. For out-of-print books, I suggest you shop on the internet at www.bookfinder.com. *Good luck and good reading!*

CDs & DVDs

There are numerous CDs and DVDs on The Ohio State Buckeyes, Coach Woody Hayes and The Ohio State University Marching Band. They cover a wide variety of subject matter and the period from approximately 1965 until the present. Again contact your favorite Ohio State Collegiate Team Logo Store for your selections.

1220
Ohio State Football
Trivia Q & A

Additional copies available from
leading bookstores nationwide.

Comments, questions, updates,
additional trivia or promotional sales?
Contact the author

Mike McGuire
27081 N. 96th Way
Scottsdale, Arizona 85262-8441

480-563-1424 tel.
480-563-1468 fax
mmcguire@fastening.com

Go Bucks!™ BEAT MICHIGAN®

AUTOGRAPHS